YOUR LEADERSHIP LEGACY

Why Looking Toward the Future Will Make You a Better Leader Today

Robert M. Galford

Regina Fazio Maruca

HARVARD BUSINESS SCHOOL PRESS
BOSTON, MASSACHUSETTS

Library of Congress Cataloging in Publication data forthcoming.

Galford, Robert M., 1952-
   Your leadership legacy : why looking toward the future will make you a
better leader today / Robert M. Galford and Regina Fazio Maruca.
      p. cm.
   Includes bibliographical references and index.
   ISBN-13: 978-1-59139-617-8 (alk. paper)
   1. Leadership. 2. Corporate culture. I. Maruca, Regina Fazio. II. Title.
HD57.7.G339 2006
658.4'092--dc22

                                                          2006020271

To Susan, Katy, Luke, Joe, Nina, and Carly

Contents

Acknowledgments

THE AUTHORS GRATEFULLY acknowledge the many people who shared their stories, triumphs, challenges, and dreams with us as we researched and wrote this book. Some are mentioned by name in these pages; most are not. Our thanks to you all.

We also extend our heartfelt thanks to our families and friends, whose unflagging support made this book possible, and to Julia Ely, Melinda Adams Merino, Kim Arney, and all the thoughtful folks at Harvard Business School Publishing, who guided the process with insight and care.

Special thanks to the members of the initial class of the Advanced Management Development Program at Harvard University Graduate School of Design, whose openness and engagement provided the impetus for this book, and to Renato Tagiuri, professor emeritus at Harvard Business School, for his thoughtful guidance early on.

Introduction

IS IT EVER TOO EARLY to think about the kind of long-term impact you'll have on your organization? Is it ever too early to think about what people will think, say, or do, after your tenure as a leader has ended, as a result of having worked with you?

We think the answer to both questions is no. It's never too early to think about the kind of influence your leadership will have after you've retired or taken a position with another company. In fact, we believe that the earlier leaders begin to consider their leadership legacy, the better leaders they will be.

Much of the time, people begin to consider the overall impact of their leadership when they're about to retire or when they're moving on to a senior-level job in another company. The legacies they've formed at work are faits accompli, and the leader, looking back, is sometimes faced with a host of unsettling *could haves* and *would haves*.

This short book proposes to turn that common behavior on its head. The central idea is that one's desired leadership legacy should be a catalyst for action rather than a result considered after the fact. Why? It's because as best as we can tell, you have only one chance in this world, so it's important not to waste it. And if recent, quarterly, or even yearly results are your only benchmark, you might accomplish only small, discontinuous wins and never have the kind of impact you could have as a manager or a leader. By contrast, being intentional about your desired long-term impact helps you both in the short run and in the long run.

This book offers lessons that have emerged from our experiences working with and talking to CEOs, professionals, and executives from a wide range of organizations, including *Fortune* 100 companies, global nonprofit entities, large banks, and small design firms. Rob's extensive experience includes working for more than thirty years with top and senior-level executives from a wide variety of organizations. For the first fifteen years of his career, he was a consultant and adviser in the world of professional services; in the past fifteen years, he has worked more closely, and often one-on-one, with high-performing senior executives from a wide range of organizations, listening to them, teaching them, and following their progress. Regina has spent the better part of her professional career listening to senior-level managers and helping them clarify their thinking, first in her capacity as an editor at *Harvard Business Review* and, more recently, working with Rob at the Center for Executive Development in Boston.

Specifically for this book, we also spoke with recently retired top managers, senior managers whose retirements were imminent, CEOs in midcareer, and a host of new leaders. (As often as possible, these executives are identified by name in the book. For privacy reasons, however, many of the executives who shared stories of frustration, or stories of hardship, have been given aliases.)

In the course of our conversations, these leaders helped us develop and refine the idea of using a legacy as a forward-thinking tool. They also helped us hone the definition of what a leadership legacy should be. We found that the more people reflected on the impact of their leadership, the less often they described it in professional or corporate terms. They spoke of the aspirations they have for the companies they manage, but increasingly they attributed importance to the one-to-one influence they might have on colleagues, direct reports, and the people in the organization at large. The more they thought, the more they also began to talk about their desired work legacies in personal terms. "I hope that my legacy at work will be the same things for which my family will remember me, and be proud of" was a common theme.

Put simply, we found that looking forward, people wanted to achieve success in organizational or performance terms. But looking back, they wanted to know that their efforts were seen—and felt—in a positive way by the individuals they worked with directly and indirectly.

We also heard, however, how difficult it is to take the time to consider such personal legacies in the course of running a company. Big-picture thinking about the long-term impact of a leader's actions—in terms of corporate growth or direction—is built into the strategic process at most companies. But the same can't be said of the long-term impact of a leader's influence on colleagues and employees, even though that's the realm in which most of the leaders we spoke with ultimately wanted to make a lasting and significant difference.

As one executive summed up, "I want my leadership to have a positive and lasting effect on the company, of course. But when I think about how I want to be remembered, or about how I would like to think I influence others, it's a very personal thing. The issue is that there isn't an opportunity to connect those personal aspirations with the day-to-day work of running the company. It's like there's a way to think about long-term performance, on the company level. And in the course of 'performing,' there are these opportunities to make a difference on a personal level. But there's a divide; there's no way to connect the two."

In practical terms, this book's first goal is to bridge that divide. Most senior managers well understand the intrinsic link between daily behavior and long-term impact. That understanding, however, is usually implicit. The structure we propose in this book—what we call legacy thinking—makes the link explicit. Legacy thinking is a tool through which leaders can filter and assess their decisions. It provides the kind of perspective that rarely makes it to the table in the course of the daily pressures of running an organization. It also serves as a powerful check to help leaders ensure that their priorities—personal and organizational—are reflected in their actions.

This book's second goal is to help great leaders leave positive legacies. Successful companies almost always have strong leaders, but sometimes organizational success comes at a personal price. All of us can name people who built financially successful companies at the cost of personal relationships or their own satisfaction. We can also name people who excelled at driving a company forward but left peers and direct reports vowing, "I'm never going to behave that way." Did they produce positive results, in terms of the organization's success? Yes. But they left negative leadership legacies.

When top managers leave in their wake strong companies and individuals who can perpetuate that strength in a positive and healthy way, the result is both leadership and legacy at their best. Ultimately, that's what we'd like to help leaders achieve.

—Rob Galford and Regina Maruca
August 2006

Part I

Making Leadership Last

CHAPTER 1

Building a Legacy

Impact, Duration, and Judgment

I am acutely aware that all projects have short and long-term connotations. And sometimes . . . the focus tends to be on the short term. But the more quickly you can move off of that focus inside your head, the better off you will be . . . I'm not implying any slowdown in terms of thought or action. What I'm talking about is, as a leader, having the same intensity and drive, the same level of quick decision-making and execution, infused with an awareness of the long-term effect of an action or decision on the people and the organization around you.

—Farley Blackman, Vice President, British Petroleum

IF YOU ARE A LEADER—of a company, a department, a division, or any group of individuals—you will leave a leadership legacy. It won't be a record of how you behaved or a report card of your company's performance (although that is how it might be summed up by the press). Instead, your legacy will be revealed in how your colleagues, employees, and others think and behave as a result of the time they spent working with you.

If you start thinking about your leadership legacy now, rather than just before you change jobs or retire, you will greatly increase the odds of leaving a legacy that reflects your best qualities, as well as the elements of your leadership that you would like to see embedded in the fabric of the organization you leave behind.

More importantly, you will be a better and happier leader for the effort. In clarifying what you would like others to take away as a result of having worked with or for you, you will gain a better understanding of yourself in your role as leader, and you will better understand how the big-picture view of your role is fueled by your actions on a daily basis.

Your legacy is today. In a nutshell, that concept is what this book is about.

LOOKING FORWARD BY LOOKING BACK

Most of us never deliberately attempt to learn much about the full scope and scale of our influence at work. Our legacy is something we think of only at the end of our tenure at a company, or when we're on the cusp of retirement. What's more, when we do look back, we often measure success in broad terms of corporate growth, strategies fulfilled, or processes set or changed. We sometimes see how our work has influenced others, but only if the examples are obvious and publicized in the media (Gillette CEO Jim Kilts, Mattel CEO Bob Eckert, and other Kraft alumni reflecting in their work some aspects of the methods of former

Kraft CEO Mike Miles,[1] or prominent former GE executives reflecting Jack Welch's style in their next endeavors).

The problem is that this conventional approach leaves a lot on the table. The approach we recommend, which we call *legacy thinking,* shouldn't be relegated to the last stages of your turn at leadership. Instead, it should be a catalyst for action—a frame through which you reconcile your strategy and organizational vision with your own instincts and tendencies.

In the process, your legacy becomes a much more personal concept, and it marries the one-to-many nature of leadership with the one-to-one reality of day-to-day work.

Consider the people you see every day in the course of your work. Your words and actions are having an effect on them. You are encouraging them to take creative risks (or discouraging them from doing so). By your example, you are teaching them that certain aspects of running a business are more important than others. You may be showing them the highs and lows of being passionate about your work, or you may be showing them how awful it is to feel trapped in a job you can't stand. Either way, these people leave their desks each day and return home with a more complete picture of you. Each day, they also leave their desks with a more complete sense of what you are doing for them, or to them, in either a positive or a negative sense. Over time, their behavior is likely to be shaped in some manner by yours.

There is a connection to be made between these streams of personal influence and a leader's desired effect on the overall organization. But most often, leaders don't recognize that connection explicitly. When you do recognize it, you can use legacy thinking to become a better leader.

Legacy thinking does a great deal for you as a leader:

- If you're the kind of leader who tries to take on too much, legacy thinking reveals to you where your influence is actually having a lasting effect, and where it is not. When organizations are in crisis, or even when the complexities of day-to-day operations reach a peak level, leaders often take a scattershot approach, firing at anything that moves. Thinking about leadership in the context of your legacy helps you establish—and reestablish—priorities.

- Legacy thinking locates you in the history of your company, a benefit that can be particularly valuable for early leaders. Roger Lang, who retired as an executive vice president at Turner Construction after more than twenty-five years, put it this way: "If you think of the history of your company in a linear fashion, along a timeline, you can place the founder at one end, and early top executives, chronologically, along the line . . . You can also place yourself at those points, and you can begin to see the scope of your work in a different way. You start to see your potential legacy. You look at the person the company hired ten minutes ago . . . and you can see how the way they are going to work has already been shaped or framed to an extent by the people who came before. You can see what you might do for that person, and you can also see what you might do for that person *in the context of the organization you're both a part of.*"[2]

- Legacy thinking helps you recognize when you are wasting your time in a given senior management slot and also helps you identify when it is time to make a move. When leaders have to make wrenching decisions—for example, when an entity's survival is at stake—a focus on legacy pays off. (Think of the top managers at Fiat in the early 2000s, who had to wrestle with the thought of exiting the automobile business, which they had once led in all of Western Europe.)

- Legacy thinking helps you put the important task of succession planning in perspective. By revealing your natural *role* (which has little to do with the requisite responsibilities of the *position* of leader), it helps you let go and even helps you seed the success of your successor.[3]

Perhaps most importantly, legacy thinking tempers your necessary focus on the tasks at hand with a sense of greater purpose. It embeds your work with meaning that goes beyond one more sales visit, or one more management meeting, or one more deal.

LEGACY IN THE CONTEXT OF VISION, MISSION, AND STRATEGY

Legacy thinking is not a substitute, or a synonym, for a leader's organizational vision, mission, and strategy. The literature on strategy and leadership is replete with such terms as *vision, mission, purpose,* and *intent*. All these words have connotations of deep meaning, the long term, and the far horizon. Legacy thinking has similar connotations. But vision, mission, and strategy are all grounded in the organization, whereas legacy thinking is grounded in the individual. Legacy thinking guides the process by which vision, mission, and strategy are attempted. It frames a leader's set of actions and interactions in their pursuit so that the leader and the organization both emerge satisfied.

Put broadly, legacy thinking helps leaders conceive of (or refine) their visions of themselves as top managers, and their goals for their companies, by providing an honest look at their own strengths and limitations, desires, and aversions. John Kotter has argued for many years that the responsibilities of leadership encompass vision, direction, alignment, and motivation.[4] Viewing leadership with a legacy perspective helps leaders decide how best to allocate their time and attention to those responsibilities.

Legacy thinking also helps leaders understand how the trajectory of their personal aspirations may differ from the trajectory of the company's strategy. This realization enables leaders to either reconcile the difference or part ways at the right time and for the right reasons.

THE PHOTOMOSAIC: AN ANALOGY

Let's look at an illustration of how a leadership legacy complements, but does not replace or usurp, a corporate vision, strategy, or mission. Consider a *photomosaic:* an image made up of many other tiny images. In extreme close-up, you can see each individual piece, which is complete on its own; when viewed from a distance, all the pieces together create a distinct whole. This art form is increasingly popular. You can see it, for example, in student yearbooks, where an image of a school building is made up of tiny pictures of all the students' faces.

Now picture a photomosaic of your face, one that is made up of numerous individual pieces: the faces of every person who works for you or with you, along with community connections, competitors' faces, and a few other "tiles" thrown in for good measure. The cleaner and more consistent your leadership legacy, the crisper the photomosaic, with the tiles clearly forming the larger image. The less clear or more conflicting your legacy, the more blurred, or distorted, the image.

As a whole, the photomosaic of your face has little to do with the organization's goals or performance. But it has everything to do with the approach you take to leadership and the way your employees and other constituencies respond, relate, and replicate (or reject) that approach (see exhibit 1-1).

(Another, equally valid photomosaic might show the company's flagship product, headquarters, or brand logo, representing

EXHIBIT 1-1

Leadership legacy as photomosaic

the company's vision, mission, or strategy. In that picture, the leader's face might be only one of many tiles. Or it might be reproduced on several tiles, thereby representing the leader's level of influence. But it wouldn't be the whole.)

Consider Dave Thomas's lasting influence on the company he founded. In early 2005, Wendy's was the victim of fraud; a customer planted a segment of a human finger in her bowl of chili, "discovered" it, and attempted to sue the company. An investigation ultimately proved that Wendy's was in the clear, but the company went through an extremely rough period, financially and emotionally. CEO Jack Schuessler, writing about the ordeal later that year, said this: "It might have been expedient to pay off the accuser in an attempt to end the media onslaught—after all, that is the preferred form of capitulation in this trial-lawyer-driven age; but we *never* considered this option. Instead, we focused on helping the police uncover the truth, while standing behind our employees and protecting our brand. Wendy's founder, Dave Thomas, believed that a reputation is earned by the actions you take every day, and that's still our credo."[5]

Thomas, who died in 2002, left a powerful leadership legacy that guides company behavior even today. Schuessler summed up that legacy in only a few words, but his comments reflect the many streams of influence that Thomas had—over colleagues, direct reports, other constituencies, and even employees who joined the company long after he was gone. A large part of Thomas's photomosaic is clear. It has also proven to have a lasting impact. Yet it has little *directly* to do with the company's products, mission, growth rate, and the like. It is Dave Thomas, the person, reflected in the faces of the people touched by his leadership.

It's ironic that Schuessler described Thomas's definition of *reputation* much as we describe *legacy*. This idea—that the day-to-day and the one-to-one are inextricably linked with the whole—resonates at Wendy's.

Someday, far into the future, your leadership legacy may be thought of as a single image. But as it is being formed, your legacy is a multifaceted, multidimensional prospect because organizations are made up of many individuals, and an overall impact is built on the basis of many impressions and interactions. Legacy thinking, in other words, aspires to build a coherent photomosaic of the many streams of influence you have as a leader. (For an example of one small stream of influence that had great effect, see "A Small Action, a Great Effect.")

A Small Action, a Great Effect

A dozen years ago, Fred Sturdivant was Mark Johnson's boss at the MAC Group, a consulting firm based in Cambridge, Massachusetts. Mark, a graduate of the Harvard Business School, had been a quick study, becoming a senior vice president of the Group by the time he was twenty-nine. After a few years, he left the company to take a position as a senior executive at a fast-growing high-tech firm. He also got married and started a family. He and Fred stayed in sporadic contact. They exchanged holiday cards and an occasional phone call.

Now Mark was dead, at age thirty-eight, of a congenital heart defect. Sturdivant, attending the funeral, was seated a few rows behind Mark's wife and baby daughter.

continued

Fred was only half-listening to the eulogy, somewhat lost in his own thoughts of Mark's too-short life, when he heard his own name. He looked up. Mark's father, gesturing to Fred from the podium, was saying what a profound influence Fred had been on Mark. Fred had really helped Mark find himself, and Fred had "rounded him out" and given him the kind of help he'd needed to live up to his potential as a manager and leader.

Fred was astonished. He remembered that when Mark had joined the MAC Group, there had been a certain casualness about him that didn't resonate with the image generally associated with a top management consultant. But Fred also remembered that Mark clearly hadn't needed any coaching in terms of his intellectual or ethical development. He recalled that he had spent a little time with Mark "offline," offering gentle pointers about dress and professional presence. But he hadn't thought of those brief conversations as significant.

After the funeral, Fred approached Mark's father, thanked him, and admitted he'd had no idea that his influence on Mark had been so profound. "Oh yes," he recalls Mark's father saying. "You had an incredibly positive impact on him; he often spoke of how you taught him the real protocols for being a top manager. You even taught him how to dress and how to carry himself."

Much later, Fred told us that he'd been doing a lot of thinking about his role as a manager and leader after Mark's funeral:

I was always reluctant to offer what might be construed as "personal" advice to the people who worked for me. I remember talking to Mark about business suits once; and I remember a few other conversations with him along those lines . . . but I was very hesitant about doing it.

*It's one thing to offer guidance in a general sort of way,
at a staff level, maybe describing a desired work environment or setting certain standards for how one treats
clients. It's another thing entirely to do it on a one-to-
one basis.*

*Had I known that that kind of one-to-one exchange
was valuable, I might have done more of it. I will do more
of it now. Not that I'll seek out instances in which to offer
personal advice; I just won't hold back as much.*

*I guess I didn't realize the difference that something like
that could make.*[6]

Because of Mark's tragic death, Fred Sturdivant got a glimpse
of something most of us never get to see: one of the more subtle streams of his leadership legacy. What's more, he got that
glimpse in time to realize the potential importance of something he'd never before given much thought to.

Fred has written numerous marketing books. Currently in
his sixties, he continues to teach marketing at the University of
Florida and the University of Cincinnati. He sits on the boards
of numerous public companies. He knows that his students and
the other constituencies he advises value his knowledge of
marketing, strategy, and organizational dynamics. But now he
also knows that his insights into some aspects of individual
development have value. In some cases, possibly, they have
great value.

Fred has not changed the course of his career as a result of
this new knowledge. He doesn't feel the need to offer personal advice at every turn. But he allows himself a little more

continued

freedom; he no longer automatically censors himself, thinking that this kind of personal feedback is inappropriate. He has received confirmation that his instinct in this area shouldn't necessarily be curbed. He has learned that another piece of his photomosaic is probably welcome, and even needed, in his work environment.

A PRACTICAL UNDERSTANDING

It's easy to grasp the broad concept of a leadership legacy. Legacy is the enduring impact leaders have on the people they work with. It is the way that leadership lasts. It can be seen in the thoughts and actions of the people who have worked with or for you long after your professional affiliation has ended.

A practical understanding of a leadership legacy, however, is more difficult. What kind of impact? Impact on whom? Short-term? Long-term? Big? Small? When we drill down on the concept of a leader's impact, each answer seems to raise more questions, and the topic grows into an amorphous mass.

One way to begin to break down the concept and understand it in a more practical and actionable way is to think of it in the simplest possible terms. Consider this: a leadership legacy is the impact you have (that is, the scope and scale of your influence on others) over the duration of your time in a given position or at a given company, all colored by the judgment, or guiding principles, that you apply most consistently to your decisions.

We use this definition when helping leaders think through their approach to building a leadership legacy. It provides a map to the concept and guides you in using legacy thinking as an effective tool.

We also use it here as a map for this book. The chapters that follow take each segment of the definition in turn. Chapters 2, 3, and 4 consider a leader's impact. Chapter 2 discusses where your impact is felt and how you can identify the ways your behavior is already having an effect. Chapter 3 discusses a leader's natural roles compared with his or her position and job responsibilities. Chapter 4, the heart of the book, outlines how you can set the specs for your desired impact by writing a legacy statement.

Chapters 5 and 6 consider the duration of a leader's legacy. Chapter 5 focuses on the ways a leader can pressure-test a desired legacy, and chapter 6 focuses on actionable steps.

Chapters 7 and 8 focus on a leader's judgment. What pitfalls stand in the way of leaving a desired legacy? Which battles should you fight? Which should you avoid? What are realistic expectations for achieving a legacy? How can you see, and measure, the fruits of legacy thinking along the way? What does a legacy in progress look like?

Leadership legacies cannot be neatly specified or described. They can't be measured for individuals by using a standard benchmark. But they can be deliberately pursued. This definition provides a common approach that grounds the concept and allows leaders to plan and measure their efforts to the fullest extent possible.

AN INITIAL ROADBLOCK

For a few fortunate people, thinking about legacy is easy. By nature, those people enjoy making the leap between the details of the day-to-day and the broad outlines of the big picture; the discussion ignites them, and they are energized by the challenges of linking the immediate with the down-the-road and sorting out the nuances in between.

For many people, however, just the word *legacy* is daunting, even within the focused context of work. There's no way to separate the concept of a legacy entirely from overall life hopes and aspirations, and overcoming this hurdle can be tough.

This truth was reinforced for us when we scheduled our first round of interviews for this book. One of the people who had originally agreed to talk with us is a prominent individual with a distinguished thirty-year career in the senior levels of government and academia. This person's resume includes high-level government appointments, international commissions, university deanships, and endowed professorial chairs.

We had a series of conversations about the topics of legacy, but just as we were about to begin the detailed interviews, the individual paused and, finally, with great passion, said, "I just don't think I can do this. I'm afraid that my successors in certain roles will read this and find it distasteful. I think it might come across as arrogant, or unrealistic, or self-promoting. It's just too hard. Wouldn't it look as if I were full of hubris even to try to describe what I think my legacy is? I'm not sure I can do this in any case. I'm not sure I can be that honest with myself about what I hope to accomplish, or impart to other people."

These heartfelt objections, random as they were, kept on coming. And it became apparent that the topic of legacy had, for her, stirred up many unresolved issues. It called up questions of mortality, of uncertainty about how and whether the achievements to date were enough, of how her achievements, or body of work, might be viewed or regarded by others, and of what remained to be accomplished. The topic had created a tremendous amount of pressure.

There was really no choice except to take this person off the hook and free her from what looked like too painful a path. But then, a few hours later, we reconvened and talked some more, and she shared an extremely moving story about a highly regarded federal judge. This eminent jurist was an extraordinarily modest man who avoided the trappings of power and prestige throughout his career. He had endowed his children with a deep sense of public service, and they had enjoyed distinguished careers as well. In a quiet conversation late in life, he described his role on the bench as follows: "I am the defense, between the individual citizens of the country, and the masked power of the government."

It was a powerful statement and yet one this man had never uttered publicly, for fear of coming across as too grandiose. And that was precisely what our interviewee was struggling with: how do we keep our legacy in mind, keep it front and center, help it dictate our deeds and our days, and yet not let it corrupt us or delude us, or make others recoil in disgust when we articulate it or reject it as we try to act on it?

The answer is that this work can be as private or as public as you want it to be.

You don't have to go wildly public with your aspirations. You don't have to publish them in the company newsletter, and no one is asking you to self-disclose in a way that strikes you as personally distasteful. But if you at least reflect on the legacies you would like to leave and engage in some thinking about what you can do to get from here to there, you'll have made an important start. At some point, at some time, having those thoughts clear will serve you well.

Too Soon? Too Late?

That same person who shared with us the story of the judge also cast her struggles with the topic in terms of timing. "I'm too young to do this," she said. "Or maybe I'm too old."

Later, we discussed the implications of either extreme. For younger leaders, there's a serious possibility that one's desired legacies will change over time, as the individual matures and becomes more self-aware. For older leaders, there exists a danger that the process of thinking about legacy will expose regrets over roads not taken. At either extreme, legacy thinking can be unsettling or unfulfilling. But for all the people in between, and even for those at either extreme, the potential upside is greater.

Consider the reactions to the concept of legacy thinking among a group of senior executives from the real estate industry. They were a smart and successful bunch, assembled for an executive program at Harvard, and Rob (one of the authors of this book) had the pleasure of working with them for a number of sessions on a variety of topics broadly categorized as leadership. As you can imagine, an extensive, if not excessive, number of topics fit under that umbrella, and he considered the topic of their legacies among them. So as part of their work together, on the eve of the last day of the program, he asked them to compile a legacy statement—a reflection describing how they wanted to be remembered—as part of their leadership self-examination.

Early the next morning, shortly before the final sessions began, one of the popular members of the group beckoned to Rob and said, "I think you may have wasted your time in asking the people in this group to fill out a legacy statement. It makes sense for someone like me, twenty years older than the average person here and close to retirement, but for the rest of them, I'm not sure it makes that much sense. They're in the middle of their lives, worried about refinancing mortgages, removing personal guarantees, building wealth. They're not focusing on things like their legacy and what they want to be remembered for."

Rob asked him whether he would mind if Rob tested that assertion with the group, asking them up front about the topic's relevance to their needs and their current existence. The man agreed, and when the class started, the two recounted their conversation. The intensity of the reaction surprised both of them.

They heard what can best be described as an outpouring of personal testimonies—story after story from people in their thirties, forties, fifties, and sixties, describing the impact and meaning they hoped their lives would have. Extremely successful people from all over the world talked about the importance of their work and described how this process of determining one's intended legacy was among the most important tasks that one could face.

In follow-up conversations a year later with several of the attendees, we found that the topic still resonated. As some of them noted at that time, a thought process not unlike legacy thinking is triggered naturally when a crisis occurs (a life-threatening illness, taking over a parent's business, and the like). But the kind of thinking that follows a crisis is driven by emotion, and, although it is powerful, the behavior changes it inspires are often not sustainable. Engaging in legacy thinking in the absence of a crisis, on the other hand, fosters cleaner insights and results in changes that are sustainable. "You shouldn't need a crisis to get that kind of clarity," one manager said. "In fact, it's probably the responsibility of leadership to act as if a crisis of some sort has already occurred, for the company's sake and for yourself."

"How Did I Do?"

Legacy thinking doesn't guarantee a successful company, and this book does not attempt to provide a strategic recipe of any kind. As Wharton professor Roch Parayre has said, "There is a difference between good decisions and good outcomes."[7] But young or old, new leader or seasoned, legacy thinking can help good managers leverage their strengths and aid struggling managers in gaining perspective.

George Colony, chairman, president, and CEO of Forrester Research, based in Cambridge, Massachusetts, summed it up in this way:

> I had never thought about the work I do on a day-to-day basis in terms of legacy . . . For me and for most people, legacy is you're out on the golf course in Florida and you're 82 and you say, "How did I do?"
>
> But I want to make great decisions every day. At the end of the day, I want to look back and say that I made more good decisions than bad ones. I want my decisions to agree directionally with the company's mission. I also want them to sit well with me as a person. If framing how I think about what I'm doing in my day-to-day work life in terms of legacy helps me make better decisions consistently, and along those lines, then legacy thinking is a very useful tool.
>
> The trick, I suspect, is not letting long-term thoughts take away from your ability to act upon the issues of the day, while at the same time acting every day to build a legacy.[8]

AN INITIAL EXERCISE

The bulk of this book explores the process of legacy thinking. It can be useful, however, to engage in the following brief exercise early (and often) to get a sense of what legacy thinking entails and how it can be used in a practical way on a daily basis.

Before your next meeting of any kind, take a few minutes to answer the following questions. What do I want people to think, feel, say, or do as a result of this upcoming interaction? Why?

Then ask this: How can I provide what they need?

Finally, ask this: If I had not done this exercise, would my anticipated behavior at this meeting be different?

Keep these questions in the back of your mind as you begin chapter 2. There, you'll learn ways to assess the impact you're having on your colleagues right now.

Part II

Impact and Duration

CHAPTER 2

What Kind of Impact Are You Having?

Getting Multiple Perspectives

ONE OF THE FIRST TASKS in planning your leadership legacy is to figure out, to the extent that you can, the kinds of legacies you are seeding now. Where are you having an impact on others' behavior or views at work? How is someone doing something differently as a result of working with you? Can you locate the influence you might be having on your immediate peers, your direct reports, and the employees who work for you outside the inner circle? Are the images in the photomosaic forming a portrait you recognize?

You can't precisely pinpoint these streams of impact, but you can get a fair sense of where you stand. One way is to cast your own performance reviews in the light of legacy thinking. This method can be particularly effective with the results of a well-done 360-degree review. Ask these questions: What do these results suggest about the effect I'm having on the people around me? How do the results place me in the context of the organization's history? What behaviors might I be introducing to or perpetuating in the organization? What kinds of behaviors might my strengths and weaknesses be seeding in other people?

Another useful approach is to participate in something we call a *multiple perspectives exercise*. In two or three paragraphs, describe what you think the major streams of your legacy might be, either at your current organization or at one you left recently. Then ask two people who have worked with you, from different parts of that organization, to provide their own brief accounts of what they think your legacies are.

This exercise is not meant to take a lot of time, nor does it need a great deal of forethought. What it does require is an effort, on your part, to think of your legacies in an active sense. The tendency is to think along the lines of "I'd like to be remembered as . . ." That's useful to a point, but it does not get at the heart of a legacy. Leadership legacies, as we see them, are not passive; they're active. They are less about image than about effect.

This exercise never fails to uncover or highlight at least a few insights. In some instances, the themes are gratifyingly echoed in the third-party accounts. In others, those accounts reveal unintentional legacies that are sometimes positive and occasionally disturbing.

Realistically, though, this exercise does not reveal much in the way of criticism, even constructive criticism. It is not a performance review; it is not a formal, organizational measure.

You're asking direct reports or colleagues to do something offline, and they probably won't use the assignment as an opportunity to point out the influence your faults have had on them. Most likely, the multiple perspectives will either affirm your own thoughts about a personal strength or will surprise you by identifying a strength you didn't know you were passing along. Generally, response essays in this exercise mention negative legacies only if they reflect a conflict in a manager's life that has since been overcome.

THE MULTIPLE PERSPECTIVES EXERCISE: CASE STUDIES

Following are two case studies of multiple perspectives exercises. You'll see that the managers and the third parties did a fairly good job of maintaining an active legacy perspective. In some cases, however, they adopted the default passive approach, considering a legacy as "something to be remembered for" rather than "something that changed the way others think and behave." Nonetheless, the results provide the desired indicators, and these are good examples of the size, shape, and content of a useful multiple perspectives exercise.

Case Study: Sally Green

Executive Vice President
Federal Reserve Bank of Boston

I have been at the Fed for a very long time—three times, in fact. It is a quality organization with wonderful people and an important mission. Even so, at times I have considered other opportunities. But then I say, "Wait a minute; I haven't yet had the impact that I want to have on this organization."

I want to influence the culture of the bank. I think the culture has begun to change, but we still have much to accomplish. The number one characteristic that I think applies to me is "engaged." I would like to see everyone of the six hundred people who report to me wanting to come to work in the morning because they're engaged with the work that they do, and with the vision of the bank overall. It's hard for people to see opportunities in an environment where there has been significant downsizing. But there are huge opportunities here, and people who connect with their work, and who understand how important their contributions are in the greater context of the organization, can see those opportunities.

One way to foster engagement is to encourage people to learn from one another on the job, and also outside the organization, outside the banking industry. Intellectual curiosity may be my weakness, because it can be the source of many distractions, but at the same time it's also the source of great energy.

Before I worked at the Fed, I was at ABT Associates, a consulting firm. I worked crazy hours there. Then my husband and I were in a serious car accident, and I was laid up for three months. When I came back to the office, all the papers that had been on my desk (and had to be dealt with "immediately") were still there. That's when I learned it's the people who are important. You choose to work the number of hours that you do. The accident forced me into a better balance in my life and my thinking.

Now I rarely carry over vacation from one year to another. Meanwhile, though, I'm probably also known for my energy. I think sometimes people below me are dying because I'm running so fast at work. I hope I influence their drive, but we also remember to have fun.

PERSPECTIVE: STEVE WHITNEY
Senior Vice President
Federal Reserve Bank of Boston

What have I taken away from Sally, as a result of having worked with her?

I think she has forever raised my expectations of myself, and of the people I work with.

Her expectations are high—so high that I think my overall performance is boosted upward as a result. I need to run harder, to keep up with her at the speed at which she runs. And I think that when I'm no longer working with her, I will still have a higher "base pace" in my head because of the example she set.

I have worked for Sally in a number of roles since 1994, here at the Boston Federal Reserve. I would suggest that there are four major characteristics that describe Sally's approach to her work, and her resulting impact on other people.

1. ENERGETIC. Sally is by far the most energetic person I have observed in senior management at this bank. She has used this energy to accomplish much, and she has this reputation now throughout the bank. While this quality is a very positive one, I would offer that at

times, it can be a bit draining on those who work for her. The saying "She has never seen a project she didn't like" comes to mind . . .

2. COMPASSIONATE. Sally has a reputation for being both supportive of her staff, as long as they perform, and of being very compassionate. By this I mean that Sally has always made it clear that a work–life balance is critical and that sometimes you need to worry about personal matters first, before work.

3. DRIVEN. Similar to energy, but here I'm describing how she applies herself to her work. She does so in a very driven manner, with high self-expectations concerning results.

4. PERFECTIONIST. Sally has little tolerance for work that does not meet her standards. Writing is the most obvious example of this; while she is known for her particular style and high quality, not many can write for her (in some cases, people don't want to write for her). She is known for taking drafts and redoing them completely to her own style and standards. This might be an example of an unintended legacy.

Sally and I have developed a working relationship based on mutual respect and trust wherein I can push back at her and know that she will at least listen to my case. Conversely, she knows that she can provide criticism to me and that I'll accept it. I have tried to portray here some of the qualities that are very positive, along with some candidness. I hope that my underlying respect for her comes through.

PERSPECTIVE: CYNTHIA CONLEY
Vice President and Associate General Counsel
Federal Reserve Bank of Boston

Here are some summary thoughts about Sally and what I think she stands for:

- Champion of new ideas and leading management principles

- Action- and results-oriented; "dynamic"

- Assertive, aggressive, power-seeking

- Decisive

- Adept at bringing affected parties to the table and identifying and achieving concerted end game

- Thrives on challenge—tough issues, tough people

- Outstanding ambassador of Federal Reserve payments principles and system

- Effective at breaking down walls and barriers

- Energetic, passionate, and devoted to tasks at hand

- Very supportive and respectful of her staff; cares about employees

- Systematic thinker, planner, and implementer

- Quick to act/react (on rare occasions, perhaps too quick, but receptive to push-back)

- Customer-focused (occasionally overreacts to customer feedback)

- Able to handle an enormous workload, but also has a tendency to overextend herself because so many issues interest her

- Often late for meetings

Here are some thoughts about how things have changed as a result of Sally's fairly new responsibility for HR:

- HR is more effective and better represented "at the table." HR has a louder voice. (Sally herself has gained a better appreciation of the importance and role of HR.)

- Sally is able to make things happen faster at the top for the HR function. (By the same token, her fast pace has made already very busy people have to work even faster and sacrifice some quality.)

- Sally has been a welcome broker and HR ambassador with respect to top executives. She has made me, and my officer colleagues in HR, more hopeful about some business propositions and HR matters. We feel more supported.

- She has brought a more systematic focus to major HR projects.

- There is occasionally more than necessary low-value, "process" work that can delay the deliverable, but that seems to be dissipating over time.

- Sometimes it can be like a tornado when Sally is "on the move"! But more often than not, that is a good thing.

Case Study: Fredric Bernstein

(Co-chair of the Entertainment, Advertising,
and Media Practice Group)
Manatt, Phelps & Phillips

*Fredric Bernstein has been an attorney and media executive for
more than twenty-five years, including serving as president of the
Columbia TriStar Motion Picture Companies, overseeing the business and operations of Columbia Pictures, TriStar Pictures, Sony
Pictures Releasing, Columbia TriStar Film Distributors International, and Sony Pictures Classics.*

If there were one phrase I'd like to be remembered for, it
would be "fair and decent." Was I always fair and decent?
I don't know. But I certainly like to think so. I always say
to my children, "I don't care if you're rich or poor, the
smartest or the dumbest, but I do want you to be fair and
decent. That's not the pinnacle goal, but it's what you
should be doing all the time." There is a line in a movie
where a man who is leaving his wife says, "I haven't cheated
on you. I've never abused you or the children. Isn't that
enough?" And of course it isn't enough; it's just how you
should be behaving every day. It's the minimum standard.

We all want to be thought of as smart, but to me it is
more important to be thought of as wise and moral and
fair. Obviously rainmaking is important, but I have told
other lawyers in my group to think about the clients they
take on. You have to pretend that you are going to have to
tell every client who the other clients are. You don't want
to have to be explaining away certain awful clients. A
potential client once wanted to hire us for a particular

assignment, and he said, "I'll have a hundred thousand dollar retainer check on your desk on Monday." I said, "I'm not sure I want it." The man then said, "I haven't told you what it's for!" And I said, "I'm not even sure I want to know." You have to be able to explain yourself.

In this business, the demarcation line that many people have between work and home disturbs me. At work it's "screw your neighbor; business is business; take the last buck." Yet at home you spend your time being pious. That is hypocrisy. The entertainment business has a low barrier to entry. With either money or connections, people can get in, and as a result, if you have the goods, you can be bellicose.

I would like my general legacies to be about fairness and decency. I have been in this business for more than twenty years, and I have never had a piece of litigation about any deal I've made. This has always been important to me.

PERSPECTIVE: ZANNE DEVINE
President of Production
Beacon Pictures, Inc.

Zanne Devine's credits include such well-known films as Four Weddings and a Funeral *and* Fargo.

There are a number of Fred Bernstein legacies I can point to in the way I do things. For one, he taught me the importance of having a point of view. Fred was my first boss, and back then I would have all the analyses ready for him but I'd be reluctant to say anything. He would say, "I want to know your point of view; I want to know what you think." The idea was that many people can gather accurate figures and provide an objective analysis, but that where people differentiate themselves is by offering their own perspective on an issue. I appreciated that.

Fred also taught me always to try to have something good to say. I remember we were at an early screening for a movie and it was just terrible. And all that was going through my mind when I was watching it was, "Oh my God, this is absolutely dreadful." I spent half the time in the screening suffering in an incredible state of anxiety because of how awful it was. When the lights came up, people looked at Fred and at me. And I observed him, and I saw him find something genuine and positive to say as he gave his feedback. So even though the movie was terrible, and he let them know it was terrible, I watched him handle the situation with real elegance. He knew how to find a way to say what had to be said, yet do it in a way that it was tolerable. "Rabbi" Fred—always humane.

Now I try always to have a point of view, and I try to ask people for their point of view, above and beyond whatever figures they're providing. And I always try to have something good to say.

Perspective: Lynda Myles
Independent Film Producer Based in London

Lynda Myles, formerly a senior vice president of Columbia Pictures, is a London-based film producer whose work includes such award-winning films as The Commitments, The Snapper, The Van, Defence of the Realm, *and others. She is also currently head of the Fiction Direction Department faculty at the UK National Film and Television School.*

I was a senior vice president at Columbia [Columbia Tri-Star Pictures] when Fred was head of business affairs there; subsequently he became head of production, and I reported more directly to him in the late 1980s. I think one of his greatest legacies has to be that he showed people that it is possible to be a "good guy" in this business. You could tell he was a good guy just by the way he treated people. He was always a gentleman.

He was a very powerful guy in the industry, yet he was the most unassuming person. There were some very "traditional" deal-makers at the company who spent every second of their lives hustling and being seen at the right parties. Fred showed people that you could be modest and unassuming without giving up any power. He did things, like coaching youth sports teams of underprivileged kids, in the most unassuming way. He wasn't doing these things to show people anything, or to pretend to be someone he wasn't. He did them just because he derived great pleasure and personal satisfaction out of the experience.

The culture, in business affairs, was always loud and pushy; you could hear people screaming down the hall. Fred always had more dignity and more humor than that; you never heard him screaming.

You don't get to be head of business affairs without being tough; Fred was a very tough deal-maker, but he was tough in a way that didn't alienate people. He seemed to manage to keep a sense of himself as well. In a community where people seem always to be watching their backs, he was able to be himself and have fun.

My sense is that he provides an example, still, for good people who want to succeed in this business. His legacy is the message, widely felt, that you can succeed even in a cutthroat field like this one without compromising yourself and your values. His legacy is one of fairness. He was an extraordinarily decent human being in an industry where there are so many monsters.

Sally Green's and Fred Bernstein's informal assessments of their own leadership legacies seem to be in agreement, in large part, with the views of their third-party respondents. As the response essays reveal, however, Green and Bernstein have also been influential in a few areas they might not have been aware of previously, or might not have paid as much attention to. Green, on seeing the essays by Steve Whitney and Cynthia Conley, for example, noted that the exercise increased by a degree or two her understanding of what people need (and don't need) from her in order to do their jobs and engage in their work. Bernstein saw that his influence seems to cluster around themes of fairness and decency, but also includes authenticity, humor, and having an interest in others' input.

WHO RECEIVES YOUR LEGACIES?

After you apply a legacy perspective to your formal reviews and participate in an initial multiple perspectives exercise, it can be helpful, in locating your impact, to identify the arenas in which these possible streams of influence are having an effect.

How large is the universe of your legacies? Might some of your behaviors have a significant impact in one area (among your immediate peers) but none at all in another? Might some of your behaviors permeate from inner-circle colleagues throughout the organization? Might some reach the community in which your organization has its headquarters? Its branches?

Consider the various major constituencies who are probable recipients of your legacy. Imagine what a legacy might look like for each group, and assess why and how the legacies might take effect. Exhibit 2-1 illustrates this process.

Your Successors

Your successor is the person who takes on your title, your responsibilities, and your authority when you leave. Your successor will be affected in some way by who you are and what you've done even if he or she has never met you.

What might your legacy be for this person? It might be as powerful as a set of deeply rooted operating principles on which

EXHIBIT 2-1

The recipients of a leadership legacy

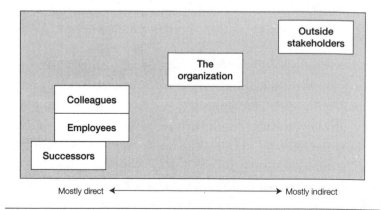

the new leader can build his own success as a leader. It might be a challenge to keep up the pace or, in times of growth, to push even harder; it might be a gauntlet. Or it might be toxic; if you leave behind a wake of political infighting or a budget mess, your successor might be forced into a turnaround role, building a legacy from that rocky starting point. Either way, your legacy can steer and enable (or limit) your successor as he begins to form his own legacies. Do you remember what it was like when you started in your role? What baggage, or gifts, did your predecessor leave, and how did these legacies affect your work?

In a world of constant restructuring and reorganization, leaders' jobs are often divided or dissolved. With the possible exception of the CEO position, many (if not most) jobs are reformatted in scale, scope, or responsibilities when a new person steps in. The successor to a senior vice president of human resources, for example, might become instead the "chief people officer," with a much broader level and scope of responsibility. If the departing senior vice president was aware beforehand that the job was going to change, she might try to leave as a legacy a solid base from which the new position could expand. A powerful legacy, in that context, might be a balanced management team with clear performance measures in place. A chief people officer starting out with that strength would be able to take on additional responsibilities much more quickly and confidently.

Contrast that example with one in which a newly appointed senior vice president would inherit the same title and job long held by the predecessor. A typical but unintended legacy might be a set of long-held expectations on the part of department members and the greater organization. They might include the level of autonomy with which people work or the amount of authority they exercise. Depending on the circumstances, these expectations might feel like a noose to the successor. An enabling legacy, on the other hand, might be deliberately crafted and delivered during the transition. The outgoing manager might offer some thoughts about where the department might be headed, what the unfinished business is as he sees it, and where the rough spots can be expected. A positive legacy would give the successor a sense of ownership ("this is your baby now; there are a lot of possibilities") and also set the tone for support of the new person within the department and in the greater organization.

Legacies picked up on by successors are often broad-based and oriented toward the nature of the job; however, they can be much more intimate if the people in question were colleagues before the transition. A former direct report who has been promoted may pick up on the schedule, or habits, of the former leader. She might use the same method to prioritize work, or the same agenda for a regular meeting. Over time, these legacies may fade away as the successor hits her own stride. On the other hand, if the legacy is very strong, the successor may incorporate it into her own way of doing things. In this manner, leadership legacies become cultural distinctions of an organization.

Employees

This group often picks up on thought processes or frameworks used by their top manager, even if they do not report directly to that person. For example, if the senior executive employs a certain approach to setting goals or running brainstorming sessions, that technique (if it's successful) is likely to be replicated throughout the organization even if it is not that executive's mandate to do so. The top manager's behavior, in this sense, is almost like a pilot program for processes and frameworks, and it may spread through the organization as other managers adapt similar approaches and move on, in some cases, to other organizations. The Jack Welch disciples mentioned in chapter 1 worked directly with the boss; they in turn probably left similar process and framework legacies to their direct reports. And so on, and so on.

Another potentially powerful legacy that employees take away from their leader stems from that manager's behavior. Employees are astute, ceaseless observers of their bosses' behavior. Sometimes, that behavior causes them to make a significant change in the way they behave in the workplace. Sometimes employees seek to emulate their leader's approach, adopting it as part of their own work style. Or employees vow, "I'm *never* going to do that," and the legacy is a group of people who deliberately do things because they were put off by their bosses' actions.

For example, Emily Nagle Green, CEO of The Yankee Group, said that she learned a great deal from observing George Colony when she was one of his lieutenants at Forrester.

> I watched George in so many meetings; I was the beneficiary of him saying, "Wait a minute. I challenge that," as he tried to get people to see beyond whatever narrow box they'd drawn around a problem.
>
> I think that I developed a reputation as the person who was always "finding another option," and I think that's in part because of George. People came to me when they were stuck, and I would say, "We can't have exhausted all of the possibilities. We're smart people. Let's sit and think; let's go to the whiteboard." I watched

George do that so many times. He has an ideas-oriented strength, and I don't see how there *couldn't* be a connection between watching his focus and my behavior and approach to work.[1]

By contrast, a senior manager at another company, recalling a period when he worked for a COO whose timing was often off, had this to say about learning from his boss's behavior:

He was a great guy, but he would make himself miserable because he was never doing the right thing at the right time. He couldn't set reasonable expectations. I watched him try to complete really complex projects in too little time. I watched him try to delegate massive tasks to inexperienced employees and then end up having to bail them out. As a result of all that, I try harder, in the office and in life generally, to make sure the project fits the people, and that there's enough time to finish things. I try to balance things better, having watched him have a rough time.

Similarly, the CFO of a chain of resort hotels told us that he is careful not to make "sweeping comments" as a direct result of having worked with a manager who did so. "This person would take a department that was functioning very well, zoom in on one negative thing, and destroy morale across the board by making a public, sweeping comment about that one particular issue. He would nitpick; he would completely miss the big picture, and it would affect the whole department in a very negative way. It's one thing to correct someone; it's another thing to blow things completely out of proportion. I try more deliberately, as a result of having worked with this guy, to keep things in perspective."

This CFO also recalled a manager who would deliver negative feedback by placing sealed envelopes in people's mailboxes. "This guy is a friend of mine," he said, "but he's a terrible manager. Think of the effect that that kind of note would have. People couldn't tell their side of the story; all they could do was feel a great sense of unfairness and frustration. Now I don't think I ever would have delivered negative feedback in that way, but as a result of working with that manager, I'm extra careful about how I discipline people. You do it in person; you set up an appointment. You don't blindside people, or take away their voices. You let them vent; anyone deserves that opportunity."

It is a quirky truth of legacy that good managers are not the only ones to leave good legacies. Unhappy managers, disorganized managers, and even just plain bad managers can leave good legacies in the form of a next generation of people who learn from their predecessors' mistakes.

As Sally Green put it, "When you walk out, what's left is people and their commitment and contribution to the organization. That's what you leave behind."

Colleagues

Colleagues can also pick up, indirectly or directly, frameworks or processes their leaders integrate into daily life at work. So, too, can they choose to emulate or avoid their leader's behavior. But this group is also likely to pick up on your baseline approach to work in general. Colleagues learn how you think about work. They come to understand what you bring to the table each day, what your values are, and what your philosophy toward work is. If your approach resonates with them, that may be a part of your legacy.

Roy Schifilliti, director of business affairs at Simmons College in Boston, told us about a colleague of his who is a cancer survivor. As she was nearing her five-year anniversary of being free of cancer, she asked him if he would ride with her in the Pan-Massachusetts Challenge, a two-day bike ride to raise money for cancer research. Here is what Schifilliti told us:

> I said yes, and I went out and got a bike and I started training for it. I hadn't ridden a bike in twenty years, but we had five months to train and I was getting myself into pretty good shape. I trained by myself, and I'd tell her what I was doing. At one point, about two months into the training, she pulled me aside and said, "You know, you're being really intense about this. You don't have to be so intense."
>
> I am really intense; I'm competitive about everything I do, at work, everywhere. But she gave me a different perspective on myself, and she showed me that I was missing part of the picture. After that, I started training with her. She had lost part of the muscles in one leg to the cancer; her pace is different from mine. But I realized that the whole experience of training was so much more enjoyable because I was doing it with her at her pace. And what I got out of it was different. When it came to the race day, we rode together and it was tremendous.
>
> For me to slow down enough to really get a full view of everything was a huge step for me. But now I try to slow down at work as well, and make sure I'm getting a full view of everything. We're in different fields in our organization; she is the associate dean of student life. Her job in many ways has different demands than mine. But her approach has changed my approach.[2]

You wouldn't want or expect someone to say, explicitly: "Learn from my own personal struggle." But if the awareness that others may be "receiving" a legacy spurs someone to raise their own standards, or set their own personal benchmarks a little higher—or if that awareness gives them a reason to behave as they would have their "best selves" behave—then legacy thinking is working.

Outside Stakeholders

Among outside stakeholders, you're not likely to find people who will say that their behavior or way of looking at the work world has changed directly because of your actions. You're more likely to find people you've touched by influencing their work or community environment. The links are often fuzzier at this distance. It's increasingly difficult to distinguish between a particular leader's legacies and the influences of the organization. But it's still important for you to consider them from as personal a standpoint as possible.

For example, how closely is your company's performance linked with the economic health of the community where it's based? Sustaining employment levels in a community, or even attracting other employers, is one sort of legacy received by outside stakeholders. The actions of Leon Gorman, chairman of L.L.Bean, have had a profound impact on the citizens of Freeport, Maine. The top managers at Cummins Engine Company have a similar impact on Columbus, Indiana.

Another legacy felt by outside stakeholders might be sustaining or raising the perceived professionalism of the entity or the industry. We know the owner of one small airport limousine company, for example, whose efforts to develop an industry association have promulgated national standards for limo drivers in training and behavior.

Establishing a strong tie between a corporate entity and a nonprofit cause is also a visible example of such a legacy. Fostering an environment in which an industry can evolve more quickly or easily is another. The combined legacies of a cadre of highly talented individuals gave us such zones of industry as Silicon Valley and Route 128 in technology, and the areas around Prato and Treviso, Italy, as zones of fashion.[3]

Most top managers can't point to an evolving community or an important scientific advance as happening under their watch. When there are significant numbers of people between the leader and the impact, it is exponentially harder to pinpoint the legacy. But these legacies are no less important. Small-business owners play an important role in the vitality of their communities every day. The challenge is to understand how your influence travels and changes as it moves from a more-or-less direct path to an indirect path.

EXPECTED IMPACT, UNEXPECTED INFLUENCE

In their 1986 book, *The Big Boys*, Ralph Nader and William Taylor wrote, "People tend to gravitate towards the standards by which they are judged."[4]

That observation can present a conundrum for top managers, who have a set of given (and often public) measures they're judged on in real time. These measures are the expected impact of leadership. The problem is that, faced with those expectations, a leader may concentrate on those measures to the exclusion of the behaviors that are less publicly judged but that potentially seed significant legacies.

The exercises offered in this chapter were designed to highlight or uncover a few of those less-public areas of impact. The next step in legacy thinking hones those insights by exploring the differences between a leader's position (or title) and her natural role. Chapter 3 explains how to do that.

CHAPTER 3

What Role Are You Playing?

Looking at Your Unintended Impact

*Good Heavens! For more than forty years, I have been
speaking prose without knowing it.*

—Jean Baptiste Molière (1622–1673),
  Le Bourgeois Gentihomme

WHO WERE THE LAST TEN PEOPLE to knock at your office
door (or call or send an e-mail)? What did they want? Were they
there to get your insights on a short-term project? A long-term
project? Did they need a sounding board to help them prioritize their work? Did they need a personal pep talk? Conflict
resolution? Representation?

Were they there to seek guidance on an open-door issue, or
a closed-door issue? Did they want your judgment, your point
of view, or a particular ruling or answer?

Do these same people regularly consult you about the same sorts of problems, conflicts, or questions? Have they done so for many corporate seasons, during periods of growth and also during performance plateaus or in times of organizational stress? Have others come to you for help with the same sorts of issues?

Any themes that emerge as you consider those questions warrant your close attention. They can be helpful indicators of the type of impact you're having on the people you lead.

This chapter helps you build your base of knowledge about the nature and scope of the impact you're having on others. The people who reach out to you—outside of routine contact within the scope of your job responsibilities and theirs—can tell you a lot about the role or roles you naturally fill at work, whether or not those roles directly reflect the responsibilities of your title. For these people, you are meeting a need. In the context of legacy thinking, their needs offer another glimpse into the legacies you may be seeding, and a possible focus for the legacies you would like to build over time.

WHEN YOUR POSITION DICTATES YOUR ROLE

Sometimes, the nature of your job dictates the type of leadership skills or behaviors you need to employ or emphasize to be successful. These skills and behaviors can build powerful and often positive legacies, but not necessarily the ones that would give you the most satisfaction if you knew that they were influencing the behavior of others. What's important, in the context of legacy thinking, is the extent to which you understand where you're putting on a hat to face a particular challenge—and where, absent a crisis or situation that requires a particular style, you're most at home.

Edgar Bronfman is a good example of a leader whose position dictated his role for a significant time. Bronfman became CEO of Warner Music Group after its buyout from Time Warner. He garnered praise for bringing to the company a collaborative, co-operative, and rational management style that resulted in a dramatic improvement in performance. But when Bronfman first became CEO, his style was reportedly quite different. He quickly and decisively reduced costs by $250 million, in part through extensive layoffs, and his actions were met with much skepticism, internally and externally. Bronfman likely could not have created this new culture in the organization that existed the day he stepped in. Only after his initial strong actions could he begin to rebuild the executive team and nurture a culture that wasn't based on fear. (In the political arena, this type of approach is often referred to as a "Nixon in China" strategy.) What's more, before Bronfman joined Warner, he had moved Universal's Seagram and music units into part of Vivendi, taking a lot of heat for the perceived less-than-stellar results of that entity. It is possible that Bronfman's legacies from his previous job shaded people's initial impressions of his actions at Warner Music Group.

Michael Ward, a managing director at Bain Capital, provides another good example. He told us about a man—we'll call him James—who had an instinctively gentle management style and whose strength lay in motivating people by giving new purpose to their jobs. Hired as CEO of an ailing consumer products firm, James initially had to wear a very different hat. He came to believe, within the first two months on the job, that a big part of the company's problem was the poor performance of many of the people one level down from top management. Most of these managers had been with the company for a long time. But before James could begin to act on the vision and strategy he had for the company, he needed to fire fourteen or fifteen of them and restructure their divisions. James had been hired for his ability to conceive of and implement long-term growth plans as well as motivate employees, but his initial impact did not reflect those qualities. In fact, employees did not recognize or appreciate those natural strengths until the impact of his housekeeping diminished.

These two leaders possessed a variety of leadership skills and called into play those that were needed to face the job at hand. The legacies they built during their initial months on the job were just as important as the ones they fueled after their organizations were stable. From the standpoint of legacy thinking, however, what's important is where the two men got the most satisfaction from their jobs, and whether they were able to identify and articulate those areas.

As a leader, you need to adapt to the situation at hand. As a person attempting to plan the way you influence others' behavior, you need to be clear about how you instinctively influence others. The chance of successfully building a particular legacy increases if your instinctive behaviors complement your goal. Put another way, the legacies you aspire to create have a greater chance of taking root if they play to your natural role or roles.

IDENTIFYING YOUR NATURAL ROLES

There are many good and valid ways to lead; three people, given the same job, can certainly succeed even if they have differing management styles and philosophies. Natural tendencies can also be influenced and accentuated, revealed or hidden—a degree here, two degrees there—depending on the circumstances. But when you plan viable legacies, your goal is to align your intent with your instincts as closely as possible. As Mark Twain wrote, "A man cannot be comfortable without his own approval."

In that spirit, consider all the environments in which you've held leadership positions, and define your roles in each one. The idea is to articulate clearly your natural roles, as distinct from your career path, your current position, or the condition of your company.

There is no template to follow; this isn't a formal exercise. Instead, it is a big-picture assignment whose goal is to distinguish between your roles and your titles, to identify the areas in which you derive the greatest satisfaction and possess natural strengths, and to home in on the areas in which you might want to focus your legacy planning.

In researching this book and asking a variety of leaders to identify their natural roles, we found that a few broad categories emerged. These are not mutually exclusive, nor do they apply to everyone. You might see yourself described to a *T* in one category; more likely, these descriptors offer a point of reference for your assessment.

Ambassador

Ambassadors instinctively know how to handle a variety of situations with grace. They tend to be the person who diffuses nasty situations, and they often get involved in conflicts on behalf of broad constituencies and not for their own benefit.

Following a long career as a consultant, Jon Younger became the chief people officer at National City Corporation, a large Midwestern bank. In his capacity as chief people officer, Younger introduced a host of people-assessment and development frameworks to an organization that previously had few such tools. Other organizations have had great difficulty introducing such frameworks, but at National City, the employees seemed to easily understand and accept the new order, and most of them point to Younger as the reason. He has the natural ability to break new ground without breaking glass.

Interestingly, Younger did not have home field advantage. Most of his colleagues at the bank were from the region, as were most of the employees, but Jon grew up in Brooklyn. Still, his ability to be persistent in a gentle way—to be persuasive and at the same time respectful—saw him through.

If you think that you have ambassadorial tendencies, ask yourself, Do I like breaking new ground without breaking glass? Do I find myself acting as the go-between when a conflict arises? Am I an instinctive problem solver? Am I the one who bridges gaps at meetings? Am I the one who interprets and placates? Am I the diplomat in negotiations? Am I usually holding and pointing the spotlight rather than standing in its beam?

One executive we interviewed for this book, a highly regarded expert on postmerger integration, cites Indra Nooyi and Steve Reinemund as good examples of natural ambassadors. Nooyi is president and COO, and Reinemund is CEO, of the merged entities of Pepsi and Quaker. "These were thoughtful people who figured out how to deal with and integrate a whole host of complex issues, not the least of which were organizational," he said. "If you consider the complexity of a merger of two such powerhouses, each with significant assets, brands, and histories, it is no mean feat to lead organizations through such a combination. It becomes a testament to those individuals, if not a legacy in and of itself, when executives can bring companies through that kind of change and still have a reservoir of good will remaining."

Advocate

Advocates instinctively act as the spokesperson in a group. They tend to be articulate, rational, logical, and persuasive. They also tend to be relentless (in the positive sense of the word), championing ideas or strategic positions. Advocates often use both linear and nonlinear approaches when they argue a point.

Alice Milrod, for twenty years an investment management executive in Philadelphia and most recently a senior executive in the private client and investment management businesses of PNC Bank, thinks of herself as a natural advocate:

> We did a big project recently. We introduced managed accounts for the bank. It was one year in the planning and nine months of execution leading up to the rollout; it involved more than one hundred people. I spent a lot of time telling people beforehand what the concept was all about; I explained in detail to people who really didn't have to know detail in order to get their work done. But I always want to make sure that people have an opportunity to contribute, and you can't contribute unless you fully understand what is going on, and you are encouraged to contribute.
>
> I hope, as part of my legacy, people will know something more than they might have about harnessing the

organizational skills to pull off such a large project . . . I'd
like to think that my natural strengths have to do with
encouraging diversity as a concept, throughout the organization. I am passionate about that. There's a tendency,
when someone doesn't understand what another person
is saying, to shut that other person out. I feel the burden
is on me to figure out what they are trying to contribute;
it may be incredibly valuable. I'd like to be remembered as
someone who facilitated diversity, and diversity of thought.
And if I can set an example for anyone else to follow, that's
where I'd like to make an impression."[1]

George Colony of Forrester Research is an advocate at heart,
although he is also someone who created a company. Colony
believes fervently in the power of technology. He is passionate
about using technology to improve the way companies do business. In retrospect, he says, he took on the role of builder, in large
part, to create an arena in which he could excel as an advocate.

If the role of advocate is familiar to you, ask yourself, Do I
tend to rally for a cause at work? Am I generally unhappy with
the status quo? Do I have a passion for excellence? (On the
downside, have I been called a perfectionist in a negative way?)
Do I see the need for redress, and, when seeing the need, am I
compelled to act?

Top managers who are natural ambassadors may do very
well at navigating through rough waters. But for advocates,
being in rough waters is part of the reason they revel in their
work. (Many advocates tend to see things in black and white
only. Ambassadors, on the other hand, can generally spot
nuances in everything. That's why advocates often need ambassadors on their senior management teams—to help them tem-

per their messages and persuade employees to buy into their decisions.)

People Mover

People movers are talent spotters and career builders—people with parental, nurturing qualities. They instinctively take the lead in building teams, and they're natural mentors. They usually have large contact lists; they are constantly introducing new people to new ideas and new paths. They're also mindful of their employees' lives outside work; they view performance through the larger lens of potential.

Sally Green of the Boston Fed sees herself as a people mover. "People might see me in a variety of roles, including ambassador and builder," she says. "And I have to an extent participated as all of the above. But the most natural—and the most important—for me is the role of people mover. Helping people build their own careers. I want to influence the vision and the culture of my organization, and I see the best way to do that is through the development of people to their full potential."[2]

If you think you are, at heart, a people mover, ask yourself, Is this the area where I get the most satisfaction? Do people continue to rely on me for career advice, even after they have left the company? There is a certain holiday-card joy that comes with being a people mover; when people continue to update you on their progress because they know you'll care, even if you have nothing in common with them and are effectively out of touch with them, you know you're a people mover.

Interestingly, advocates may find themselves in people mover roles, but the key distinction is that developing people is not where they reap their joy.

Truth Seeker

Think fairness, good judgment, a sense of equality, level-headedness, process orientation, scrupulous neutrality, and objectivity. The role of truth seeker is the only one for which there is a prerequisite: truth seekers are unfailingly competent in their field, and their competence is unquestioned.

Truth seekers instinctively level the playing field for those in need. They also help people understand new rules and policies. They act to preserve the integrity of processes, and they try to identify root-cause, or pivotal, issues. They also step in to ensure a just and fair outcome if the process has failed to yield it.

Successful individuals in the human resources function are usually naturals for this role. Truth seekers also tend to gravitate toward line-manager positions.

Jim Rossman, COO of a large advertising agency, cited Joanne Zaiac as an example of a truth seeker. Zaiac is the president of the firm's New York office, which employs more than five hundred people; Rossman has been a member of her leadership team. Rossman explains why this executive is an example of a truth seeker:

> Joanne solicits rounded, open feedback. She drives to outcomes but shows great flexibility by saying things like, "If we don't have enough information to make a viable decision, we'll go out and get more." She always makes sure there is enough information. For example, when she was new to the job, she created a hundred-day plan . . . She set up a series of morning breakfasts and invited specific people across a broad spectrum of the office to attend,

to gain their perspective. That approach in both shaping the office agenda and implementing it is characteristic of how she works, and it's one of the aspects of her style that is rubbing off on her colleagues and on the people who work for her.[3]

Tom Leppert, CEO of Turner Corporation, the parent of Turner Construction, offers another example: Turner executive vice president Stu Robinson. A substantial number of regions report to Robinson, and, as Leppert puts it, "Stu is consistently highly objective. You can rely on that. He is not just analytical, but objective. He has a natural ability to figure out the essence of a situation. What are the two or three critical factors here? What is really important, versus what is clouding people's perspective?"[4]

In one instance, a dangerous set of conditions began to emerge on a project—conditions that, if mismanaged, could have had far-reaching implications. "Stu stepped in, literally over a weekend, brought the parties together, and reinforced their common objectives," Leppert said. "He was instrumental in guiding the various constituencies—the owners, members of the community, the contractor, the subcontractor—through a process that resolved the conflicts. I see general managers and other Turner people trying to emulate that quality. When they're dealing with conflicts, they're thinking, 'What would Stu do?'"[5]

Russ Lewis, retired CEO of the *New York Times,* essentially described the truth seeker role when talking with us about how he ultimately hoped to be thought of by colleagues and employees: "I would like to think that someone might say, 'If I had to trust somebody with a judgment, I'd like to see Russ up there in the jury box. He may not be a brain surgeon, but he tries to do what's fair. He never makes decisions based on politics.' I'd like to think that they might say, 'That guy was a mensch. When we needed someone to stand up for something, or make an unpopular decision, he didn't run away.' If I thought I could have a significant influence on the people I work with, I'd want to see that quality carrying forward."[6]

(Interestingly—and gratifyingly—when we asked several of Lewis's colleagues to describe his legacy at the *New York Times,* and his effect on their own approach to work, their descriptions of him matched what he told us.)

Truth seekers keep people in the game; they keep people enfranchised, and, as a result, their employees are less likely to engage either in passive aggressive or openly adversarial behavior.

If you believe that being a truth seeker is your natural role, ask yourself, Do I have a strong sense of justice? At the same time, do I have great sympathy for the underdog (and do I act on my feelings)? Am I attuned to the importance of symbolic gestures? Am I good at spotting the root cause of a problem or conflict? Am I not satisfied unless I believe I have identified the root cause of a problem or conflict? Am I occasionally accused of being too rational too much of the time?

Creative Builder

These individuals are visionaries and entrepreneurs, driven (and happiest) at the start of things. They instinctively see new opportunities for new products and new companies; spot niche markets; take ideas and make them real. They're often serial entrepreneurs over time, even if they remain in one leadership post.

Creative builders instinctively understand that building is not necessarily about invention but about the process of implementing an invention. Builders are constantly energized by new ideas, and yet they have the staying power to see them through to fruition. The issue is rarely simply the idea; builders aren't "Hey Mike, what's your latest scheme?" people. Rather, builders are fascinated with implementation. Real estate developers are often creative builders in this way as well as literally; they feel most rewarded when a project gets under way or is newly completed.

Builders sometimes get into trouble if they remain in one place for too long. There are case studies, too numerous to mention, of entrepreneurs whose legacies are negative because they became enmeshed in the day-to-day operations of the companies they created and didn't know when it was time to leave. Builders can successfully remain in a single leadership position only if they figure out how to feed their own need for new projects.

Rob Cosinuke, an executive at (and former president of) Digitas, a Boston-based marketing services firm, is a good example of someone who understands that building is where he gets the most satisfaction: "I guess I see parts of each role in myself. It would be an aspiration for me to be an experienced guide. But if you ask other people (and if I really ask myself), I am clearly a builder. I have ten projects going now; I always have ten projects going, at work and at home. There's a new offering in the business; I'm building shelves; I'm forming an alumni association. Maybe it's a form of antidepression to have so many things going; it's definitely what I get my energy from—building new things, creating new things."[7]

Here's an equation to try on yourself if you identify with the role of builder:

Strength of belief in end result + Ability to tolerate
the process = Creative builder

Experienced Guide

The term *experienced guide* conjures up an image of someone old and wrinkled, with the experience that comes with age. That's not incorrect, but experienced guides don't have to be old, or even necessarily experienced. What they must have is an ability to listen and to put themselves in others' shoes. They have a way of helping people think through their own problems; they are natural therapists. Often, they are seemingly bottomless wells of information on a diverse range of topics. Experienced guides are the people who can always be counted on to supply the right quotation or the right historical connection.

They are not necessarily mediators, and yet experienced guides often find themselves in the middle, with people on both sides of a conflict seeking advice. When a corporate meeting has been stressful or fraught with conflict, the post-meeting, closed-door meeting often takes place in the experienced guide's office.

Remember the family lawyer of old? The person outside the family who knew (and kept) all the family secrets, and was often sought for advice? The experienced guide role naturally lends itself to the position of minister, counselor, or trusted adviser.

Renato Tagiuri, professor emeritus at Harvard Business School, noted that natural experienced guides are often found one level down from the top in organizations. They get their greatest satisfaction by helping others get through the day and helping others see the bigger picture. They empathize.

THE BENEFITS OF GAINING INSIGHT INTO YOUR ROLES

Once you've identified the role or roles that you believe you most naturally fill, it's useful to test them by looking for objective supporting evidence. Start by listing a few of the ways your chosen role might manifest itself at work. Are these actions that you come by naturally? If so, great. If not, ask yourself why not. What is limiting your ability to fill the kinds of roles you would like to fill? It's possible that your selections are slightly off course. If there is no marketplace demand, it is possible that the role you'd like to play isn't aligned with your abilities. In that case, you need to reexamine the range of roles you identify with and assess whether your aspirations are clouding your perceptions of your strengths and weaknesses.

At the extreme, an increased understanding of your role can help you determine whether your position offers the alignment you need if you are to be satisfied over the long term. Consider the executive—we'll call him Paul—who in 2004 accepted the job as president of a national brokerage firm. Paul was flattered to be offered the job and rightfully pleased to accept the position. But many of his colleagues feel that he would be happier as a superbroker (his longtime position prior to his current job). He has not been Peter-Principled; by all accounts he is doing a good job as president. But there exists a clear perception by many of his peers and direct reports that Paul is fighting an internal battle over whether he should remain in the job.

At leadership levels, the opportunities to let natural roles emerge often are limited by the regular demands of the position or by situational circumstance, such as the holiday selling cycle, an intense period of work resulting from a merger, or a significant new-product launch. All these things factor in to the mix of required and voluntary things you do each day. It's true that the day-to-day demands of leadership can easily obscure the kinds of avenues a top manager might prefer to pursue. It is also possible to free up time to do more of the kinds of things that make your job ultimately rewarding.

We work with a CEO—we'll call him Matthew—whose travel schedule is so intense that it crowds out most of the chances he has to step back and reflect or to counsel younger members of the organization, as he would like. The daily demands of Matthew's job play to his strengths as a builder in the sense of organizational and market growth. But they don't allow him to be the people mover he also would like to be.

Matthew knows that he is good at envisioning and articulating a long-term strategic view. He knows he is good at motivating and mentoring younger executives. He knows that his time is invaluable in their eyes. In rare free moments, he meets with these people, answering their requests for general guidance and pep talks. Yet Matthew finds it difficult to incorporate that mentoring into what is already an overloaded schedule. His typical six-day workweek might include a trip to California, a trip to New York, and a forty-eight-hour stay in Germany.

Does Matthew have "an issue" delegating work? It's possible. More likely, the structure of his top management team isn't optimal. His company doesn't have a chief operating officer, for example, even though it has grown substantially in the past thirty years, and that void clearly warrants attention. (Recent articles in the press have highlighted a lack of COOs in large corporate organizations, so his situation is probably not unique.[8])

Recently, however, Matthew has made some progress in incorporating more of his would-be role as mentor and visionary into his job, despite the organizational circumstances. As this book was going to press, his company was preparing for its second internal leadership development course for midlevel managers, a course staffed and taught by senior managers. He has now built into his formal schedule two three-day events each year designed to allow up-and-coming managers the face time with him they crave (and, by the same token, to allow himself to "indulge" in the kinds of mentoring behaviors he rarely has time for otherwise).

Matthew is well aware that he needs to address the design and structure of his senior management team. In the meantime, he has found a way to make his working life more enjoyable in the short term and to seed a legacy that he knows he wants to leave for the long term.

This CEO is also a good example of the ancillary benefit of having an increased understanding of one's own natural roles. He has begun to identify others' natural roles as well and, in doing so, is better able to temper the advice or counseling he gives. He is also better able to calibrate his senior management team: understanding the roles that dominate the team now, Matthew is seeking people who will instinctively help the team gel and become more effective.

A colleague of ours, considering her natural role in her organization, said, "It is a luxury, in a sense, to be able to identify and home in on one role at work. As a parent, you can't say, 'Sorry, honey, you know, I'm more of a builder/creator. You'll have to deal with that teen angst elsewhere.' You have to give it a shot. But at work, if you see something heading your way that doesn't play to your strengths, you can divert it. In fact, you'll be rewarded if you bring people into the organization who can handle the kinds of things you're not great at."

THE LEGACIES YOU ADOPT

As a final step before we turn to the exercise that lies at the heart of this book—writing a legacy statement—it can be useful to investigate the concept of impact from one more angle: the impact of other leaders' behaviors on you.

Consider what William F. Schulz recalled about the influence of previous directors on his job from 1985 to 1996 as head of the Unitarian Universalist Association. (Schulz retired as the executive director of Amnesty International USA.)

> There were key predecessors of mine who left very significant legacies that shaped the way in which I approached my work. The first president after the merger of the Unitarian and Universalist churches, for example, set a benchmark for the largeness of the presidency. He was a builder and creator type of person. He was most comfortable working at conceptual levels. He raised the visibility of the position, and also brought a degree of seriousness to it that had not previously existed. Even though I became president some twenty years or so after his tenure, the nature of his presidency and the way in which he had formed it was still very evident. He had seen the leadership job as being visionary rather than passive. He had envisioned a strong executive president. That dimension of seriousness had diminished since the end of his presidency in 1969 to the time I became president in 1985 but I still felt it strongly. I wanted to renew the organization's sense of itself as a serious player in the world. The legacy I took from him was the way in which I came to understand my position.[9]

What legacies have you received from others, and how have those legacies shaped the way you lead or want to lead? What were your bosses' natural roles? Did their legacies to you stem from those roles, or from a disconnect between their natural roles and their behavior?

By extension, do you think their legacies formed a clear photomosaic portrait? Or were they more likely to be fragmented, their portraits blurred, as a result?

In chapter 4, we nudge the nature of legacy thinking from an investigative process to one that reflects your aspirations. You will identify the types of legacies you want to build, whether or not they align with the legacies you are creating now.

CHAPTER **4**

Your Intentional Legacy

Writing a Legacy Statement

What will you do with this one wild and precious life?

—Mary Oliver,
　　winner of the Pulitzer Prize and the National Book Award

ONCE YOU HAVE A SENSE of the types of legacies you may be creating and you have assessed your natural tendencies along those lines, it is time to write a formal legacy statement. If you're purposeful about building a legacy, this is an essential step. A legacy statement is a way of setting the specs for the kind of impact you want to have at work. It also makes the concept of legacy thinking tangible by giving you a benchmark.

Writing a legacy statement goes beyond describing the actions or symbols of accomplishment that you are most proud of. Instead, your legacy statement should focus on your behaviors, values, or approaches to leading and managing. If you could see your organization ten years from now, or fifty, what aspects of your leadership would you like to see still in play?

Far from being a prescription for the legacies you are confident you can leave, a legacy statement should describe your aspirations and direction. You'll be asked to answer a short series of questions thoughtfully and realistically, but also hopefully.

Vivek Paul, president and CEO of Wipro Technologies, told the following story in *Fortune* magazine: "The best advice I ever got was from an elephant trainer in the jungle outside Bangalore. I was doing a hike through the jungle as a tourist. I saw these large elephants tethered to a small stake. I asked him, 'How can you keep such a large elephant tied to such a small stake?' He said, 'When the elephants are small, they try to pull out the stake, and they fail. When they grow large, they never try to pull out the stake again.' That parable reminds me that we have to go for what we think we're fully capable of, not limit ourselves by what we've been in the past."[1]

That same sentiment applies here.

Your legacy statement requires more consideration than the multiple perspectives legacy exercise offered in chapter 2. That was a quick hit to get you oriented; this one, in contrast, requires at least an hour of uninterrupted, solitary time, and possibly more. (A few people who have completed it describe it as a perfect airplane activity.) Ironically, though, the statement will likely turn out to be shorter than the document you may have prepared for the multiple perspectives exercise. Let's go through it step by step.

STEP 1: REFLECT

The first step is to take a few minutes to reflect on your career path so far. In broad strokes, look back, look forward, and then look inward.

Think back to your first and second jobs—not your first and second jobs out of college or business school, but your very first teenage or summer jobs. From your vantage point as a leader, what was it like working those jobs? Do you find that your perspective has changed now that you are a senior manager? What legacies did you see from your initial leaders? How did those legacies affect you? Also, what sensory memories do you have—sounds, colors, smells? What is your general sense of the atmospheres or environments in which you worked? Did they leave a lasting impression?

Jot down your thoughts. (Don't worry about format; scratch notes are fine.)

Now think about your first jobs after college or graduate school. Ask yourself the same questions. Again, don't push, necessarily, for well-formed memories. Impressions are equally valid. Recall your sense of things, isolated experiences or conversations, your recollections of others' experiences, even colors, smells, and sounds. Stream-of-consciousness notes are fine here. The desired outputs are thematic characteristics or values that have shaped and still shape your approach to work.

For example, one fifty-something manager we spoke to—we'll call him Frank—remembers that at his job in the institutional

investment division of one of New York's largest banks, everything seemed to be gray. "The walls were gray; the carpet was
gray," he said.

> I can also tell you that starting with the memory of that
> grayness leads my mind to reflect on the general atmos-
> phere of the place. Individuals did not spend a lot of time
> conversing . . . People rarely shared much of themselves,
> beyond work issues, in those halls. To its credit, I recall,
> the place was not particularly political; it was a place
> where good work got done, and where there was mini-
> mal conflict. But at the same time, it wasn't a beacon for
> creative types . . . Two men who left the organization . . .
> created an early-stage venture capital firm and made tens
> of millions of dollars in record time.
>
> It was the kind of a place where you would look at
> the clock and it would be 3 p.m., and then you'd go back
> twenty minutes later and it would be ten minutes of 3 . . .
> When I decided to leave the job, I wrote down on a
> piece of paper "Just Remember the Pain," and I marked
> the date on it . . . Everyone was telling me I was foolish
> to leave such a promising, secure career track . . . My
> salary, at $20,000, was more than my father made, but I'd
> taken the job for the wrong reasons. My note to myself
> was intended to remind me, no matter where I ended up,
> that staying for the money and stability wouldn't have
> been worth it. I kept it in my wallet for years.
>
> My efforts to create organizations that are stimulating
> places to work for every employee are likely due in part
> to my experiences at that rather gray place. I didn't make
> the deliberate connection between that bank and my

approach to work until I began to explore the concept of legacy thinking as a leadership tool. But I think, subconsciously, I have been trying not to recreate that atmosphere in every organization I've been a part of since then.

The owner and president of a small business provided another good example of the types of recollections that can be part of the prep work for a legacy statement. When he attempted to reflect on early jobs, the following memory popped into his head. He wrote it in shorthand for his own purposes; here is how he described it to us:

It was my first day on the job as an associate. It was a low-level position, but I'd been led to believe that it was a career track job, and that it was expected that people would move up quickly. It was about 10 in the morning, and I went down to the little kitchen at the end of the hall to find out if there was coffee available for employees. There was a coffee machine, and I asked one of the more senior people who was standing there if the milk in the refrigerator was for everyone to use. I remember that he shook his head, at first, and then said that a group of people took turns buying the milk. I asked if I could join the group, and said I'd be happy to buy the next bottle. He said, "Well, I don't see why not, but we'd better run it by the other folks, to make sure no one minds. You probably shouldn't take any right now; let's just go ask." He also confided, dropping his voice, that there was better coffee at the other end of the hall, in the little area just outside of the executive suite, but that the coffee there was "by invitation only."

I remember thinking how strange this guy was, and how odd that we would spend so much time on something so trivial that had nothing to do with the work. It didn't occur to me at the time that he was conveying the entire culture of the organization in this little talk about milk.

But now, looking back, that's exactly what he was doing, and that example can sum up for me the kind of culture I try to avoid building where I work, and the kind of culture I aspire to create. As it turned out, the position I was in was *not* on a growth track; most people at that level, including myself, left the organization within a few years, sometimes much sooner. The feeling we got was, "Not good enough to be one of us, not good enough, not good enough," [but later, when people left,] "Oh how can you leave us? You were so good; you were going to the top here!"

The culture there was that if you had to ask a question, you weren't very smart, and you certainly didn't have the authority to make a decision about anything on your own, no matter how small it was. I saw it reflected in the words of the person who couldn't tell me whether it was okay to put milk in my coffee. But I also saw it in meetings. People in entry-level "career track" jobs were expected to be quiet . . . We had weekly division meetings; after every one, there was a series of closed-door meetings throughout my department. People always had to dissect what had been said; someone always needed comforting.

I find myself, today, having reflected on all of this, using the word *milk* as an unspoken cue to myself. I try to ensure that no one is intimidated at my organization. I try to let people know that their contributions are welcomed. I know that sometimes people are going to have naïve perceptions of a situation; maybe they don't have the experience that a more senior level manager has. But I also know that you don't gain that experience by skulking around in the background, too afraid to do anything.

That same guy who couldn't say yes about the milk also told me at one point during my first week on the job to "trust no one." Now, I could riff on that for a long time; that statement says worlds about the place. But it's also more obvious, and it could lead people to think that there was something wrong with that particular employee. There wasn't. He was highly productive, creative, thoughtful. He was a great guy. He may seem paranoid . . . but he wasn't. Working at that place probably just had the same effect on him as it did on most other people, unless they got out quickly.

Everyone has these stories, or impressions, in their work history. Unless you are sixteen years old or on the cusp of your first job, you have this kind of data; all it takes to mine it is the time and the willingness to relive the past for a few minutes and extrapolate, a little, about the long-term effects those impressions or events have had on you.

STEP 2: FIND THE THEMES

The next step is to prune and prioritize your reflections. The idea is to look through your notes and draw from them a few major themes that apply to you today.

Try to sort your thoughts under three headings:

- *Characteristics (who you are).* Who are you as a result of the experiences or impressions you wrote down? As a result of your early jobs, are you more or less something? Determined? Persuasive? Sensitive? Insecure? Secure?

- *Values (what you hold in high esteem).* Which values mean the most to you? Loyalty? Trustworthiness? Fairness? Industriousness? Which values do you look for in colleagues or direct reports? Which values do you encourage?

- *Manifestations (what shows up in your work).* How do those characteristics and values reveal themselves in your behavior at work? How have they revealed themselves this past week? This past year? If the world were a newspaper, what letters to the editor have you written?

We know of a rabbi who made the decision to say, "Look, I'm always so busy talking about how important Israel is; I should really be there." He subsequently gave up being a rabbi in the United States and opened a bookstore in Israel. The manifestations you identify here don't have to be as extreme, but they should have significant meaning to you; they suggest the outlines of the legacies, already in progress, that you may want to emphasize going forward.

As you begin this process of listing and sorting, think back to the self-discoveries, if any, that you made in reading chapter 3. Are the themes that are emerging here in sync with your perceptions of your role? If not, why not? (If not, are you being honest with yourself about your natural tendencies and aspirations, or are you posturing? If you're posturing, why are you posturing?)

Here are a few prompts to help you get your thoughts in order:

Aspirations. What got you to this point? Do you have an understanding of your own motivations? Is it reflected in the career you have chosen?

Intention. Look at the roles you have chosen or pursued. Do they match your aspirations, or is it more, as playwright Claudia Shear wrote, that you find yourself "blown sideways through life"?

Empirical data. Where and how do you actually spend your time? Does it match your aspirations?

Results. Where do you get repeat calls from people? Why do they seek you out? What results do you find gratifying?

STEP 3: WRITE THE STATEMENT

Now that you're armed with what may seem to be an unwieldy amount of data, albeit prioritized, it is time to turn to writing your legacy statement. Use the questions provided in exhibit 4-1 as a guide. Your aim is to solidify your thinking and to be as specific as you can about the leadership legacies you want to leave.

Remember that you are not writing a to-do list, nor are you creating a report card template on which you will be judged when you retire. But you are setting standards for yourself, and the hope is that you will take them seriously. Be evocative, not declarative. Record aspirations that are achievable; don't sandbag

---

EXHIBIT 4-1

Leadership legacy statement: going beyond the tangible

Writing a legacy statement goes beyond describing the actions or symbols you are most proud of. That is the stuff of obituaries. Legacy statements focus more on the characteristics and values for which you would most like to be remembered.

Creating a leadership legacy statement entails a number of steps:

1. Reflect.
2. Find the themes in your reflections.
3. Write the statement.
4. Elicit reaction.
5. Revise.
6. Occasionally review and update.

Questions

1. How do you wish to be remembered as a leader by those inside and outside your organization, both in your current role and in your career? For which two or three personal *characteristics* (or *skills, behaviors,* or *values*—pick the word that works for you) would you most like to be remembered? How would you like to have these characteristics manifest themselves? How will they show up? You might want to briefly describe a situation or even a recollection of you that someone might have in the future.

2. What have you learned in this role, your work, and your life thus far that you would most like to pass on?

3. How will you convey that learning?

4. What remains to be accomplished? Why is that important in building or completing your legacy?

5. Aside from more time, what will help or impede you in completing what remains to be accomplished?

---

yourself. Make your desired legacies a stretch, in other words, but not a strain or an absurdity.

You are also selecting and formalizing the arena in which you'd like to see your legacies grow. Earlier we noted Kotter's definition of the responsibilities of leadership: vision, direction, alignment, and motivation. Acknowledging their importance and the investment you must make to fulfill them, ask yourself what aspects of those responsibilities keep you coming to work each day. What is it really all about for you? Again, the distinction between position and role is critical. Your title may be chief financial officer; your role may be advocate. You may be a line manager; your role and legacy may fall into the realm of motivator or experienced guide. Your desired legacies may center on one organization, or they may span several. They may center on customer relations, or they may center on employee growth.

The different types of legacies spawned at professional service firms provide a good example. One partner at a consulting firm, for example, might revel in developing other consultants. Another might find her deepest satisfaction in client work. Both arenas are valid, fruitful grounds for meaningful legacies, but neither arena may reflect the position held as much as it reflects the roles filled.

Tom Valerio, a sales executive at Astra-Zeneca USA, is a good example of that last point. Valerio is in his forties. He has held senior management positions in technology, insurance, reinsurance, health care, and now pharmaceuticals. In each job he has held, no matter his title, he has helped the organization solve difficult problems and identify the right metrics for measuring and monitoring success. He has, with few exceptions, worked for leaders who have a passion for that kind of change; he is the person who figures out how to make their vision and strategy a reality. He has always worked at companies embroiled in dramatic change efforts. He tends to feel less needed and less engaged in a job after he has succeeded in stabilizing or organizing the environment and in creating the metrics the company needs so that it can move forward and track progress smoothly.

Valerio appears to be a truth seeker at heart. His legacies center, not on any one organization, but on the concepts of facilitating improved performance and performance metrics and on helping others understand how to do the same. His legacy statement would reflect a perspective based on expertise rather than on the enterprise.

It's important to understand that the question–answer format in the template does not mean that your statement must be created in essay form. You can write an essay, or you can draw a diagram; your goal is to represent your legacy in a way that is immediately recognizable to you and to other people. You might end up having drawn a series of stepping-stones; you might end up with four circles on a page, each containing a different message.

The circle format is one option we've seen work well. As shown in exhibit 4-2, you put your values and your world view

EXHIBIT 4-2

Expanding the circle

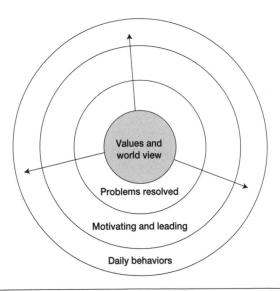

in the center, surrounded by three circles. In the circle closest to the center, describe your preferred approaches for resolving problems. In the next circle, articulate the ways you want to motivate and lead people. In the outermost circle, encapsulate the daily behaviors that are most important in light of the contents of the other circles.

Some people "think" in Word, others in PowerPoint, and others in Excel. Still others use a more free-flowing process of expression, unconstrained by or even incomparable to anything charted or programmed. It's up to you. There are no Procrustean beds here.

LEGACY STATEMENTS: THREE CASE STUDIES

Following are three case studies of legacy statements. The first is from Steve Lenox, a partner in a prominent design firm. The second is from Terri Cable, a bank executive. The third is from Carole C. Wedge, head of a major architectural firm. These statements are reproduced here because they offer a clear sense of how legacy statements differ in form as well as function. Some of them are more forward thinking in tone, whereas others are more reflective. These people deserve our special thanks for their generosity of spirit in agreeing to bare their souls here.

As you go through each statement, it may be helpful to look for the following:

- Does the essence of each person seem to emerge? Do each of the statements convey enough about the person that you have a sense of who he or she is?

- How do the writers express themselves? Do they use single words? Phrases? Stories? What does their style say to you about how you might express yourself in this format?

- How much have they struggled with the tendency to write in terms of how they want to be remembered, rather than how they want to influence others? In cases where they wrote in a more passive style, how might their words be refocused to reflect the impact they want to have on the views or behavior of others?

Case Study: Steve Lenox

Steve Lenox is a partner in the design firm Lyons-Zaremba, which specializes in providing design and architectural services for the museum industry, with an emphasis on aquarium design.

How do you wish to be remembered as a leader by those inside and outside your organization, and by those with whom you might work in the future?

CHARACTERISTICS. I want to be remembered as someone who possessed a unique blend of creative vision, technical know-how, and the personal skills to not only lead a team while fostering the personal growth of those who worked for (with) me, but to create lasting public projects as a result (we are museum planners and designers). I want to be remembered for being able to mediate and orchestrate diverse groups of people (clients, design team members, specialists, and contractors) involved with our projects that regularly require four to six years to complete. I want to be remembered for knowing when to push and when to let others do the pushing. I want to be remembered as someone who required that work be fun, especially while working on complex and demanding projects.

VALUES. I want to be remembered as someone who was a kind and generous person—someone who "put more in than he took out." I want people to remember me as a mentor and humanist. I want people to remember me as someone who enriched the lives of others. I want to be remembered as having been unselfish and without ego.

MANIFESTATIONS. I have the unique situation in my work to create public exhibits for aquariums, zoos, nature centers, discovery centers, and museums of various types. The manifestation of my life's work is in part embodied within those tangible results. They stand, in part, as my legacy. Beyond the physical, being directly involved in the development of younger staff within my firm is the most important manifestation of my life's work. More important than the legacy of my firm is the growth of talented and caring staff who will go forward with their own unique careers—careers that will hopefully see new legacies emerge, regardless of where they are employed. While the corporate image (legacy) is always important for the "moment," and is vital for the cultivation of new work, it is the legacy of people and the values they represent that will be most important to me personally.

What have you learned in your work (and life) that you would most like to pass on—for example, lessons, what to do, how to approach challenges, outlook on life, and so on?

From a business perspective, I have learned (especially in the past decade) that corporate legacy is elusive and perhaps nearing a point of marginal relevance. Corporations that have existed for ten, twenty, fifty, or a hundred years have all become more susceptible to changing markets, mergers, takeovers, and bankruptcy. Regardless of an individual's vision for the future, any corporate entity can cease to exist on any given day. I therefore focus on that which I feel can have a lasting effect, namely the people with whom I work and the quality of the work we produce.

I was raised with a very strong work ethic. I grew up in a middle-class environment, born shortly after the end of World War II. While I had the security of a comfortable life, my parents fostered in me an appreciation for working towards goals and instilled in me an appreciation for the value of money. At the core of my upbringing was my parents' desire to provide my brothers and me with the best education possible. My parents grew up in the Depression and both served in WWII. Both strove to provide their three children with opportunities greater than they had known growing up. While both supported our diverse paths in life, they probably assumed that greater financial wealth was a key part of our future goals in life. For me, while financial security is very important, it has never been the guiding principle or highest goal relative to my career. What I have learned over the years is that I had to define for myself that which was important. I came to realize that personal happiness could not be measured in dollars earned, but instead by attaining personal goals founded in my belief in people and the community(s) within which I find myself.

I find, especially today, that too many strive to direct the lives of those they are leading—be they family, students, friends, or employees. I subscribe to the notion that a good leader accepts that there may be many solutions to a given problem or approach and must be open to the possibilities that others bring to each situation. While many would argue that if you want it done right, then do it yourself, and if you are a leader, the next best thing to doing it yourself is to have others do it for you—exactly the way you would. Well, that just doesn't work in the creative process. While the immediate results may appear more in line with one's expectations, the long-term result is the stifling of personal growth and creative development of those on the team.

Thirty years ago, as a young painting student in art school, I learned how to become my own critic. Being trained as a professional artist, one had to develop the skills to evaluate one's own work, and then strategize how to improve that work. Self-awareness is a key building block to how one grows and matures, regardless of the context—be it work, family, or play.

How can you understand, mentor, and lead others if you don't even understand yourself or can't manage your own journey in life?

In today's economy and life in general, change is a natural part of life. So why do we dread it so? Those of us

raised in the fifties and sixties, we grew up with the
notion we would go to school, train for an occupation,
go to work for the company, and retire happily ever after
some forty-five years later. Now, more than ever, we must
learn to circumnavigate a myriad of changes within the
context of an economic environment that has become
increasingly harder to predict. We change occupations,
switch companies, become part of a merged workforce,
and perhaps we are the victim of downsizing. We watch as
markets shift, technologies advance, workforces globalize,
and margins grow tighter. And that's just 9 to 5! Our personal lives have undergone similar transitions. We move to
new homes more frequently, divorce at greater rates,
entertain a wider range of vices, and demand more of
ourselves and our children than ever before. It's no wonder we fear change. It's a pain in the ass! So, when considering the question of legacy in light of the increased
nature of change to our workplace, it seems that change
itself must become part of our approach to fostering
that legacy.

How will you convey that learning?

I am a partner in a small design firm providing professional services for the museum industry. My expectations
regarding conveying these lessons are shaped by my expec-
tation that our lives as individuals, and my firm as an entity,
are subject to the constant forces of change. How I will
convey what I have learned and the legacy I hope to create
are tempered by my belief that we are journeymen who
merely pass through and leave nothing more than a fleeting

impact on others. Take, for instance, the great baseball players enshrined in the Hall of Fame. Few of today's young ballplayers know who Willie Mays is. The names Jackie Robinson, Sandy Koufax, Stan Musial, Ted Williams, Ty Cobb, Hank Aaron mean little to them. Yet they led incredible careers with countless achievements to their credit. They left legacies, yet those legacies are evaporating.

What I therefore wish to convey is the importance of building a legacy that can be appreciated in the moment and the immediate future that follows. Beyond that, I believe we are kidding ourselves about the importance of who we are and what we do. To some, that may sound cynical, but I find it to be liberating. I am free to do what I believe is right for the moment and therefore become freed up from the burden of always doing the right thing for posterity. In effect it reduces the need to be remembered as an individual, but instead allows one to be remembered as an ideal—something intangible, but meaningful in others' lives. That filters into my message to younger staff, and the mentoring of their development as members of our design community. It's the same message I try to impress on my children. Having goals is certainly part of a long-range plan, but adjusting to the moment is essential for the sustenance of one's effort and enthusiasm in pursuing those goals. It's about finding the passion in one's life and worrying less about the judgment of others. More specifically, I try to lead by example and convey through that effort an approach that works for me, but while doing so, making it perfectly clear that mine is but one approach.

What remains to be accomplished? Why is that important in building or completing your legacy?

Because of my personal beliefs and values, I believe I have been building my legacy (however great or small, I cannot say) for my entire career. So on one the hand I trust that if I die tomorrow, the essence of my legacy will already be in place. With that said, I do hope to develop a greater body of work, have the opportunity to work with a wider range of designers, and be more in the forefront of new trends and directions within my industry.

I am eager to work with new people and to add something to their lives, as they add to mine. It fuels my interest in my work, as I hope it fuels the interest of those I work with. I do not perceive legacy building as something that one turns on and off like a switch. Instead it is a value system that resides deep within each of us. We choose to become who we are regardless of how conscious (or not) we may be about our choices.

Aside from more time, what will help or impede you in completing what remains to be accomplished?

To accomplish these objectives, I first must avoid playing dodgeball with cars in downtown Boston where I work. The walk between the train and my office could kill me! Second, I must nurture the reputation of my firm so that we continue to attract high-quality projects with clients of vision. Third, I must push myself to keep reinventing how it is we work so that we keep moving forward. I must strive to broaden the capabilities of the firm through the development of staff. And last, I must continue to be objective in my assessment of each step along the way so that the values that I have established for myself as a person and for my company (along with my partner) are properly tended to.

How might completing this exercise affect what you will do on a day-to-day basis, in the next week, and in the next few months?

Essentially, this exercise is a reminder to myself about the fundamental values that lie at the center of who I am, what I do, and how all of us choose (or not) to give something back to the community—be it in our personal lives or at work. As a member of a religious community where acceptance of other beliefs, and the embrace of diversity, and a call to social action are at the forefront of our community, it is common to take an introspective view of oneself as a step towards dealing with life's tougher challenges. But a legacy need not be a challenge, but an opportunity. The challenge is what we make of it. The opportunity is everything that becomes part of the process in building that legacy. I like to think of building a legacy in the same way I used to think about the George Washington Bridge. When I was a kid growing up in New Jersey, I would go into New York City by crossing over the bridge. Every time I'd cross, it seemed it was in the process of being painted. It occurred to me that it must take so long to paint the bridge, that when they got to the end, they just went back and started all over again. Building a legacy is sort of like that. Legacies are part of a continuum that preceded me, involves me, will survive me, and will eventually give way to the legacies of others that will eclipse mine with theirs (as it should be).

So, what will I do on a day-to-day basis? For me? This week? Next year? I suspect I'll be out there painting the bridge. I'll probably see you out there too. And when I get too tired to lift the brush, someone younger will pick it up and carry on. In that I trust. After all, that is why we create legacies in the first place.

Case Study: Terri Cable

Terri Cable is an executive vice president at FirstMerit Corporation, a multibillion-dollar bank holding company based in Ohio.

How do you wish to be remembered as a leader by those inside and outside your organization, and by those with whom you might work in the future?

FOCUSED, LOYAL, AND COMMITTED to results and to people and to whatever I do. Those around me get the best from me.

LEAD WITH MY HEART while demanding results and accountability. I love people and I give them all of me; however, I expect them to deliver and hold them accountable.

FEARLESS AND OPTIMISTIC. I enjoy growing, learning, and getting better at what I do every day.

SELFLESS. I am genuinely interested in others' success and development. I love to see those around me succeed and I love helping them reach their goals. I like watching others grow—through reaching and stretching and sometimes falling down. Knowing when to step in and when to step out is really important.

HONESTY, INTEGRITY, COMMITMENT TO FAMILY AND OTHERS AROUND ME. I believe that the "whole is greater than the sum of the parts."

VISIBILITY. I would like to be known as someone who was *there,* and who listened and learned.

What have you learned in your work (and life) that you would most like to pass on—for example, lessons, what to do, how to approach challenges, outlook on life, and so on?

- To be an effective leader, it cannot be about you! It is all about those around you—your family, your coworkers, your clients, and your shareholders. You can't just say it, you have to live it.

- Every good strategy requires great execution! Execution takes people!

- Let your results speak for themselves—easy to say . . . it's tough to do.

- Egos get in the way . . . leave them at home. (Don't confuse ego with confidence.)

- Actions speak louder than words. Produce at the highest level, set high standards—then go above and beyond.

- It's all about people: create an environment where people grow and develop, they feel free to make mistakes and share with others. Never ask others to do what you wouldn't do yourself.

- Love what you do—it's contagious.

- Believe you can do anything, then do it!

- Last, know your strengths and use them every day.

How will you convey this learning?

Through living it every day. In both my professional and personal life, I debrief after every meeting and after every presentation and every encounter—even if only for a moment. What can I do better, how can I be more effective, and what should I do differently next time? I am a communicator and I mentor quite a few people—professionally and personally. I convey what I have learned through my actions and by sharing and hopefully by continuing to get better every day.

What remains to be accomplished? Why is that important in building or completing your legacy?

Much more fine-tuning. As I have said several times, it is all about my actions. When I get stressed and pressed for time and deadlines, I have to stop and remember why I am here. The distractions . . . they are often the things that are important, not the board presentation or the budget meeting.

What is important in building my legacy is making a difference to others who I hope will then reach out and do the same. I want to create an environment around me that allows others to see that you can succeed in this way. Having your own agenda—in business or personally—creates a short-term focus that is generally not in the best interest of others. It is damaging to a company, an organization, or a relationship. My experience is that egos generally get in the way, and that individual agendas in the long run hurt! So that's why this is so important to me.

Aside from more time, what will help or impede you in completing what remains to be accomplished?

Me—not giving up! It does take a lot of time and energy, and as I get more responsibility I look for ways to become more efficient. I don't do what I do to make a difference—I do it because I believe it does make a difference!

How might completing this exercise affect what you will do on a day-to-day basis, in the next week, and in the next few months?

It has forced me to think through what I do and why I do it! It made me realize just how much of my life is focused professionally, and how important it is to balance my efforts and energy. So it's Sunday, and I am at work—and it's a holiday weekend. This exercise, I hope, will remind me to share myself more across all parts of my life!

Case Study: Carole C. Wedge

Carole C. Wedge is president of Shepley Bulfinch Richardson & Abbott, a national architecture, planning, and interior design firm established in 1879. Its work includes educational, health care, and scientific facilities around the world.

How do you wish to be remembered as a leader by those inside and outside your organization, and by those with whom you might work in the future?

CHARACTERISTICS. Authentic, thoughtful, good listener, realist, creative, ambitious, problem solver, fair, mentor, honest, had a real impact. Ultimately, I think I am an ambassador.

VALUES. Humanist, open-minded, ethical, honest, spiritual, enjoys life, enjoys people.

MANIFESTATIONS. Pushes for change in a fair and straightforward way, full-disclosure approach to decisions, involves others, allows people to do their best and use their natural talents. Does not let problems persist. Challenges historic patterns of work, thinking, and interacting. Asks good questions—probes the challenges to formulate robust ideas.

What have you learned in your work (and life) that you would most like to pass on—for example, lessons, what to do, how to approach challenges, outlook on life, and so on?

Life is what you make of it. Enjoy it.

It is all possible. Be yourself.

Power is an empty, soulless place. Collaborating means you get to share the success with others. It is all about people.

Finding reward in others' successes is exciting and energizing.

Listen to your heart. If you are doing something you don't enjoy, it shows.

Intellectual freedom, interest, and engagement have a lot to do with success.

Nurture yourself so that you may nurture others.

Apply all of those things to team-building and the kind of work we do.

I like to think of our business as a campfire. If you want to turn a campfire into a bonfire, you can't put the big logs on first. You have to build up the middle ground. I'd like everyone to understand how to connect the dots so that the company can grow, or scale, successfully.

How will you convey this learning?

Living it every day—by example.

Looking for opportunities to reinforce it—actions. When someone says, "What happens if we do that?" I'll say, "I don't know; let's go find out."

Being deliberate and explicit about building teams that can withstand the pressures of very diverse opinions. A colleague once said to me, "You are teaching me to think really carefully about putting teams together. You are teaching me to think a lot more about the intricacies of who is on the team and why, and the complexities that teams contain. It's not enough to have the right people on the team if you don't know how to manage the team to foster collaboration."

Talking with others about their learning—sharing knowledge and experiences. Soon after I became president, I put together a design charette [a focused architectural plan] for our own firm. We had sixty people get together over a weekend; we were together for breakfast, lunch, and dinner, and everything in between. We talked about what the firm was, where we were going, our potential for doing things. One of the senior partners came back to me later on and said, "In all my years here, this is the first time the firm has done something so inclusive and creative." He said he was inspired. Frankly, it wasn't much, but it was sufficient to make a difference. I would like to keep opening doors like that. I'd like to keep opening doors that people have never opened at the firm, or have been to afraid to open.

What remains to be accomplished? Why is that important in building or completing your legacy?

Achieving tangible results; seeing accomplishment of goals.

Seeing changes occur.

Seeing the next generation of leaders take it on; helping them get there.

It is important because it feels like the impact I can have, especially on my firm, is just beginning. The firm is at an inflection point. I want to make sure it really arrives at a bolder, more creative, outspoken place that has a creative, strong, and authentic impact on the institutions, communities, and people that are affected by our work.

Aside from more time, what will help or impede you in completing what remains to be accomplished?

What will help:

Focus.

Ability to create momentum and dispel inertia—or the natural inclination to assume change has occurred when in fact it is just beginning.

What will help is growing a larger group of like-minded people in our firm to work together and evolve the vision together.

Communication.

What will impede:

Distraction—things that are less important or remote from the core/real needs getting in the way.

Critics/negativity.

Bad economy!

How might completing this exercise affect what you will do on a day-to-day basis, in the next week, and in the next few months?

Keep the flame.

Keep the focus.

Don't be deterred by obstacles.

It will take time.

Writing this statement reminds me that life is a process and a mystery and that showing up with ambitious intentions and a respectful attitude is most of the battle.

GETTING STARTED ON YOUR LEGACY STATEMENT

As we synthesize our observations on the legacy statements that people have shared, the following points emerge as the most helpful to apply when you create your own statement:

1. Legacy statements are slightly harder to think about than actually write, but it takes less time than people think to get started. After about three minutes of internal squirming and a few comments along the lines of "This is harder than I thought," people get right down to it.

2. Don't worry about sounding too idealistic. People apologize for that, even as they create these things (there are a lot of asides, either spoken or written, such as "I hope this doesn't come across as too idealistic" or "I can't believe I'm saying this"). Life has a way of turning idealism into reality quite nicely. In this way, at least people start with high aspirations.

3. People worry about their precise word choices. They shouldn't. It's not a legal document. No one's going to test it in court. And chances are, you won't be reading it to your company from a podium.

4. It's a good measure of how closely people identify with their work, as opposed to their jobs. Legacy statements are much more about people's work than their jobs.

5. Be careful if you make a distinction between a work legacy and a nonwork legacy. The desired characteristics and values should be closely parallel, if not identical. They may manifest themselves differently, but that's to be expected.

6. People feel good for having done it. They say it helps them affirm what they are trying to do, or it gives them a little push to try something—surprisingly often, in improving an important interpersonal relationship. We're not psychologists, so we can't offer very much on that. But maybe it shouldn't be surprising that it pops out so frequently.

One of the difficulties people encounter when they're working on a legacy statement is that they come face-to-face with their own mortality. Sometimes, writing a legacy statement underscores for people how much they have yet to do. One of the things that helps them get past that difficulty is considering how their own work can seed the legacies of others. Virtually every legacy statement we've seen has included, in some form, a thought about how the leader's own passions can best help others develop their own careers and also help others create meaningful legacies.

The next chapter fosters this type of positive and forward-thinking outlook by examining how to test a statement in the context of real work and by encouraging the kind of editing and revising that will ensure its viability and resilience.

CHAPTER 5

Is Your Legacy Designed to Last?

Pressure-Testing Your Statement

ONCE YOU'VE CREATED A LEGACY STATEMENT that you are more or less happy with, it is time to pressure-test by giving it a personal reality check, and also by asking a close friend or trusted colleague to give it a read.

The exercise of writing a legacy statement represents a serious investment in legacy thinking. For that investment to pay off, the statement must reflect behaviors and goals that are achievable and realistic and, at the same time, aspiring. Your goals must also be authentic, in the sense that they must be self-driven and not tied to expectations generated by other people or constituencies.

In his seminal work, *On Becoming a Leader,* Warren Bennis wrote, "I cannot stress too much the need for self-invention. To be authentic is literally to be your own author (the words derive from the same Greek root), to discover your own native energies and desires, and then to find your own way of acting on them. When you've done that, you are not existing simply in order to live up to an image posited by the culture or by some other authority or by a family tradition. When you write your own life, you have played the game that was natural for you to play."[1]

Are you reflected in what you wrote in your legacy statement? Will your confidants see you reflected in your statement? Are your aspirations realistic? Do they appear so to your reader? Have you identified real areas of potential? Have you aimed too high? Too low? Will your reader connect you with what you've written? Or will he shake his head and say, "Get your head out of the clouds, buddy"?

This reality check is about understanding what you've written, understanding the implications of what you've written, and ensuring that it resonates both with you and with someone who knows you well.

Earlier, we acknowledged that sharing personal thoughts about your legacy can be difficult; sharing a document as revealing as this is probably as hard as it gets. Not everybody cottons to this step or embraces it with great enthusiasm. That's understandable. In part, it can seem a little self-centered (something along the lines of, "But enough about me. Let's talk about you. What do *you* think of me?"). In part, you may fear that you will be perceived as searching for compliments. In part, it can feel somewhat embarrassing or overly revealing. All that combines to make many people reluctant to share it. Lacking an external view, however, you're talking to yourself. If you don't review it with someone else, even a less than objective person such as a spouse, you're missing a bet.

Here's a telling example of the value of an outside perspective. At one executive training session, a particularly wealthy participant (owner of numerous hotels and real estate in some of the priciest areas in the United States)—we'll call him Jamaal—went through his proposed statement with another attendee, who had become a friend. Jamaal's statement included a reference to his desire to make more money. The friend asked him, "Are you really worried about money?" Jamaal said, "It still is on my mind; I still feel the need for more. I have to figure out why." It was a valuable moment for both individuals. In Jamaal, it sparked a deeper consideration of the validity of something that had provided significant motivation throughout his career. In the reader, it allowed an increased understanding of a colleague and also provided an additional point of perspective for his own legacy thinking.

The value of sharing your legacy statement with someone else is incontrovertible, because it gives you a chance to test your desired legacy with minimal risk. In addition, a second set of eyes can add insight as to whether you are missing something that belongs in your legacy—a latent or nascent characteristic that appeals greatly to others. Finally, it gives you a chance to revise your legacy in prospect.

SOLICITING AND ASSESSING FEEDBACK

What kind of feedback can you expect a reader of your legacy statement to provide? The answer depends on your relationship with this person and the seriousness with which you approach the topic. Reactions of all sorts can be helpful; possibly the most we can offer here is that it's a good idea to indicate to your reader what level of detail you would be most comfortable receiving.

The same goes for the type of feedback you'll allow yourself to give. This pressure test can be valuable when your own assessment of your document is a single flash of insight; it can also be valuable when the feedback you give yourself is more granular and you play out various "what if" scenarios throughout.

In the next few paragraphs, we offer general feedback on the legacy statements provided by Steve Lenox, Terri Cable, and Carole Wedge in chapter 4. These notes are directed in part to the writers; they also reflect the tenor of feedback you might expect and receive from a reader.

Feedback for Steve Lenox, Partner in Design Firm

The cynics among us might read Steve's statement and ask, "OK, what's he hiding?" But if he's hiding something, he's apparently doing a good job of it and hiding it from himself as well. That's doubtful, though. The authenticity of the statement is found about halfway through, when he describes his training as a professional artist, during which time he developed the skills, including reflection and self-awareness, of being his own critic. This goes hand-in-hand with the amount of perspective in evidence.

At the same time, there is evidence of some natural tensions in Steve's statement. Can one have passion and still have perspective? What mechanisms must be in place for them to coexist?

One answer lies in the sense of humor that shows itself at a number of points. Another is in Steve's lack of attachment to institutions (even his own) and his comfort with the constancy of change. He has far more one-to-one connections than one-to-many connections. There is a serenity in what Steve wrote; our sense is that it stems from the joy he finds in his work and in his ability to connect his passion closely to his career. That makes for a legacy that's easier to achieve.

If you find yourself writing a statement that contains relatively few doses of serenity and humor, how do you—to borrow a phrase—start having what Steve's having? How much of it is transferable or replicable? The answer has everything to do with the amount of intrinsic joy you derive from your work. We take issue with the contention that only those in creative fields such as design, architecture, or media find that level of joy. We have known salespeople who love to sell and researchers who love to discover, and we are blessed to live in a time when we can make choices about what we do for a living.

Interestingly, Steve focused on aspirations, realism, and stretch in one quick paragraph: "I must nurture the reputation of my firm [aspiration] . . . I must push myself to keep reinventing how it is we work [stretch] . . . I must continue to be objective in my assessment of each step along the way . . . [realism]." He hits on achievability only a few paragraphs later, as he draws an analogy between building a legacy and the endless painting of the George Washington Bridge. He finds further meaning in his own involvement in the process, as he says, "And when I get too tired to lift the brush, someone younger will pick it up and carry it on. In that I trust. After all, that is why we create legacies in the first place."

For a process-sensitive person like Steve, it might be important to push a little on the question of measures. How do you know whether you are making progress in your process? Are there particular events, milestones, or benchmarks that signify a level of achievement that would render satisfaction? Is just "keeping going" enough in the way of progress? As a creative person, Steve undoubtedly finds meaning in the completion of a worthy effort. In his building a legacy, is the process reward enough?

Feedback for Terri Cable, Bank Executive

If Terri were any more tenacious or determined, it would be hard to imagine. Her statement almost rises off the page. Focused, focused, focused. A bias for action. High expectations of herself and others. The question for Terri (and for those like her, who are similarly hard-charging, committed, productive individuals) is how to make sure these forces are tempered when necessary. We might press her to make sure she is getting enough unfiltered feedback (not only on her results, which are probably great, but also on whether her expectations of herself and others are realistic). She also needs to give herself enough time to reflect on progress and on longer-term goals, and enough time just to reflect and breathe every once in a while.

Terri provides some evidence that she is aware of the need for more reflection, more time spent on the longer term. The challenge is how to make sure she (and those like her) can and will actually do this without a precipitating event that forces it upon her.

Like many individuals in corporate roles, Terri talks a lot about results and execution. The challenge for Terri (and others) lies in the translation of the relentless requirements for results and execution into a more cohesive whole, something more than a stream of repeated quarterly achievements. Although a record of X consecutive quarters of profitable growth can be impressive, in and of itself it is not a meaningful legacy. What makes the way this performance was achieved impressive? What makes it something from which others can learn? Is it your track record that people should seek to emulate, or is it more about making sure that they know how to translate it in a wide variety of situations?

Action words permeate Terri's text (*focus, results, fearless, execution,* and so on). So do "stretch" words. But we might push Terri to be more explicit about realism. It's not that Terri isn't a realist. We wonder whether Terri takes enough time, or regularly gives herself sufficient chance, to be both objective and reflective. Successful individuals, like Terri, who fall into the category of being highly mission-driven or results-oriented sometimes benefit from a gentle reminder to give themselves some moments of reflection and the opportunity to ask themselves when and whether it is time to review or revise the mission.

Feedback for Carole C. Wedge, President of an Architectural Firm

Carole writes that ultimately she thinks she is an ambassador. Although that may be true, ultimately she is a builder. You can see it in the way she talks about building campfires, bonfires, and teams. She talks about building diverse skills and talents into teams, in almost the way one installs diverse systems into a building. That's probably fitting for someone leading an architectural firm. There is a lot of evidence of her sensitivity to both the work environment and to the process requirements of bringing people along. That comes across in her description of the way she is attempting to make change in the firm.

For Carole, her legacy appears to be closely allied to the success of the firm and its people. This is not surprising (and is somewhat reassuring) for the head of such an organization. She appears deeply committed to the organization and its people, and this takes a backseat to her own success. There is an authenticity here, an ego in perspective.

If you are someone whose legacy statement would include such phrases as "allows people to do their best" or "finds reward in others' successes," how do you pass that on? To celebrate one's work is a hard thing to do in many professional-services organizations. Carole has worked hard at that, bringing visible recognition and support for people's achievements into the ongoing practices of the firm.

Carole wrote her legacy piece early in her tenure as the firm's leader. It's full of aspirations ("accomplishment of goals . . . seeing the next generation of leaders take it on," etc.) and stretch, as one might expect. What remains to be tested, and Carole is fully aware of this, is achievability. When individuals create legacy goals at the start of a new role or stage, we should make sure to ask them to look back at the statement in a year or so. Now that they know much more, now that the job or the role or the place is no longer as locked in mystery, what is achievable? How might this kind of reflection change their legacy?

People's aspirations can and do change, perhaps because of a significant event or perhaps as a result of the passage of time or the stage in life they have reached. The same is true of what's achievable, which can (and will) change as well. That leaves only realism, which helps keep people grounded, and stretch, which helps keep people on their toes at the same time. Keeping those four criteria in constant play is what makes a legacy endure.

PARAMETERS FOR THE PRESSURE TEST

Following are a few guidelines for pressure-testing your legacy statement for aspirations, realism, achievability, and stretch.

Aspirations

In testing for aspirations, the concern isn't whether you've aimed too low. Most individuals who are thoughtful enough to construct a legacy statement, or even to imagine what their legacies might be, know that there is nothing to be gained by creating too easy a target. Few folks openly admit to hoping for a legacy of laziness. But the toughest challenge is in calibrating your aspirations and desires. There's no gain in aiming too low and no sense in aiming too high. Nor is there value in giving yourself the annoying "Shoot for the stars and you could reach the moon" pep talk.

Here's a quick test you can use, and you can ask your reader to use as well: assume success, and ask whether that is enough. If you assume, just for a moment, that your desired legacy has been achieved (example: "created a new organization that people clamored to join"), is that enough? Could you have built a better one, a more satisfying one? Would you feel as if you could have aimed a little higher? What would ultimate satisfaction look like?

The key is to do this in a way that doesn't drive you crazy; the key is to do it in a way that gives you a challenge but doesn't cause a life crisis. When people look back on these kinds of things and ask themselves, "Could I have done more? Could I have tried harder?" the answers might well be yes, but many successful people are experts at beating themselves up in hindsight.

The better questions might be, "Would it have made sense for me to have tried to do more, given everything else that might have been going on in my life? Would it have made sense for me to have tried harder, given everything else that I had going on?"

There's a big difference between these two approaches. The second set of questions doesn't let people off the hook; it puts their lives in perspective. It's far better to start building legacies in perspective than to attempt to rationalize and work through them in retrospect.

Realism

In testing for realism, look for two "rights": the right person, and the right situations.

THE RIGHT PERSON. Are you the right person for this legacy? Seriously. Do you have the characteristics that match well with your aspiration? We're not talking IQ here, or credentials or certifications. It's deeper than that. Do you have the right demeanor, the right traits, the right personality for this desired legacy tc make sense? Although you find it engaging, is it something that might be too far outside the realm of possibility for the person you are? Unless you have the answers in front of you because you are walking around with a wonderful set of freshly interpreted aptitude tests, you must figure this out. You don't need a standardized test; you do need some harsh objectivity.

For example, Dan would love to leave the kinds of legacies that builders tend to leave. He really would. The thought of leaving behind an enduring organization, product, or approach with his signature on it is extraordinarily appealing. Being regarded as a visionary sounds good, doesn't it? There's a certain appeal to thinking that people might call you a visionary even after you're gone.

Dan has often thought about building something new, especially when he was younger. He even got to the "ad in the *Wall Street Journal* and printed brochure" stage. But, builder of something? It really wasn't Dan. Wasn't then. Isn't now. He admits that he is not sufficiently possessed by the vision, not sufficiently interested in the actual process of constructing something, not sufficiently detail-oriented to want to attend to it, and certainly not patient enough to nurture it along for an extended period.

Would he still like to leave some of that builder's legacy? Sure. But if he lost perspective, would someone, in helping him test his legacy statement for realism, help him realize that following such a path makes no sense? We hope so.

THE RIGHT SITUATIONS. Even if it's realistic to pursue your desired legacy from the standpoint of skills, character, and personality, it's worth making sure that it's realistic from the standpoint of your position, your industry or company, your career path, and the like. Are you in the right situation to develop your desired legacy?

If you want to work closely with people, do your intended legacies show themselves in the kinds of activities that are highly regarded in your company? If there is less of a premium on people development and more of a premium on product or business development, is the situation right for your legacies to take root? If you are running a research laboratory, are you finding yourself devoting more time or effort to an area that drains you of energy? Is it likely that these circumstances will change?

In short, you should be testing for potential mismatches between your responsibilities and your legacy goals. What in your situation will have to change, or what will you have to change, in either the short term or the long term, to reduce those mismatches? Is it the set of responsibilities? The job? The employer? The industry? The profession? When might those things change? Is it worth the wait?

Marla is a master at sales. She has worked for an elite chain of health clubs, for a maker of fine jewelry, and for an international financial corporation, among others, and her marketing skills generate admiration among her colleagues at every turn. She is a natural truth seeker, a role that has served her well in her marketing positions; she has never been in the position of trying to sell anything she didn't fully understand or think well of.

But for several years now, Marla has grown increasingly dissatisfied with her life in sales. There is a mismatch between the responsibilities of her position and the kinds of things she wants to accomplish in her work life. Her legacy goals exceed her position; no matter how you look at it, the inevitable answer is that she must move on.

Recognizing this, she is now pursuing a graduate degree. But she regrets the time it took her to take action. "I thought about it longer than it is going to take me to do it," she said. "I don't know what I was waiting for; nothing changed."

Be wary if you hear yourself saying, "I'll be able to get started on this as soon as . . ." Ask honestly: How soon is "soon"?

Achievability

In testing a legacy for achievability, what you're really doing is asking whether your desired legacy has a chance. If it is likely to require an inordinately high, ongoing level of resource expenditure on your part (whether it is time, money, or energy), are those resources available to you? Given what is on your current plate at work and in your personal life, what trade-offs will be required? What are you willing to reduce or relinquish to help you get there?

Gene has a great job with a venture capital firm, where he provides expertise to companies in the firm's portfolio. He also has a principal operating role in one of those companies. He wants to be remembered as a builder; he wants to build the venture capital firm's portfolio of companies in his area of expertise. However, his family obligations are significantly greater than the norm. It's not easy for Gene to focus on the builder legacy that has been his goal.

The only thing that has helped is that, in Gene's words, he's just hit "the big 4-0." He knows he has too much on his plate, and he knows he must make some decisions about what he can and cannot hope to accomplish. He may have all the requisite skills and talent to be a successful builder, but that legacy goal may simply not be achievable, given his circumstances and the trade-offs he's had to make.

If you have had the time to even imagine your legacy statement, you are ahead of the game. At least you are focusing on the question. You know that achieving some or all of your desired legacies requires trade-offs. What might have to go, in order for you to get there? It's always a question of trade-offs, redirection, or elimination of activities. It's very unlikely that you are insufficiently busy or have too much time on your hands. That would be a happy problem. So what must come off the plate, and stay off?

Stretch

If you have done a good job in terms of aspirations, then the execution of your goal should be invigorating. You're doing what you want to do. It doesn't get better than that, does it? Or does it? As you envision yourself proceeding down that path, it's a good idea to examine it in a couple of ways.

First, it's worth testing whether this is how you want to spend considerable time and thought. How much stretching do you want to do? Will it invigorate you along the way? Will the endorphins kick in as you are on this run, or will it be a tough slog because the stretch itself offers little in the way of gratification?

Second, is this a good run for the longer term? How long? Not every legacy you desire at one point will make sense to you five years later. External circumstances will change, and you will, too. As fewer people stay in the same company or even the same job for an extended period, are you at a stage when you can see even a little bit over the horizon?

Consider the twenty-something daughter of a client—we'll call her Sandra—who has been working in New York for a large company. Obviously on the front end of her career, Sandra is on the cusp of figuring out what she wants, and yet she has an impressive ability to think about what she would like to look back on. She wants to make sure that her work will also be a stretch, not only in difficulty or responsibility but also in testing her instincts about which business skills she should develop over time. She knows the most important skills will not come from only one experience but from many of them.

In the eyes of those who are important to you, is this stretch right for you? Does your trusted confidant and reader understand why you want to strive for these outcomes? Do the people you love support these goals? Do your desired legacies make sense to them, even if they might not aspire to the same goals?

CLARIFYING YOUR INTENTIONS

After you've considered your statement against these criteria and have received feedback, it's time to consider whether you want to revise it. Did your reader raise a relevant issue you hadn't thought of? Incorporate it. Did she take issue with anything you wrote? If so, why? Do you see her point? Do you want to revise what you wrote as a result?

As with the multiple perspectives exercise in chapter 2, leaders are often a little surprised by the reactions they receive when they conduct the pressure test. Most thoughtful leaders can at least identify, in broad strokes, their own weaknesses. Fewer can (or are willing to) pinpoint their pockets of strength. And even though most of the leaders we have worked with are well versed in setting stretch goals, many find it difficult to align *legacy* stretch goals with the goals of their business and with the achievements that will give them the most personal satisfaction. Even a little help along those lines can have a meaningful impact.

Rob Cosinuke of Digitas likens this pressure test to having a good 360-degree evaluation performed by an effective executive coach: "I had a senior-level coach do a 360 on me, and he came back and said, 'Let me tell you about you. Here's what people love.' I heard about all these things that I do, outside of work, that people inside work had noticed and appreciated . . . It's almost as if the coach gave me permission to do this stuff. Thinking about legacy now, and about what I learned through that process, I hope that my legacies will be balanced. I hope that they'll not just center on helping people get a life at work, but on how they can do that by bringing their lives to work."[2]

The pressure test affords you an opportunity to ensure that your expectations vis-à-vis your legacy make sense. It can also give you "permission" to pursue activities and goals that you might otherwise have thought were less important, or important to you personally but not in the context of your position as a leader.

Put another way, this test opens up an opportunity to clarify your intentions. You can do this in your head, if you like. But if an exercise would help, consider the following.

WHAT'S ON YOUR PLATE?

Draw a large circle on a piece of paper. (If you have a paper plate handy, use that.) Make a pie chart of the types of demands placed on you in a typical day. Have the chart reflect the amount of time you devote to each of those demands.

Now draw a circle on another piece of paper or paper plate. Draw a pie chart of the way you wish your day were structured. Have this chart reflect the amount of time you spend on different tasks.

If you continue doing things as the first chart illustrates, can you project how you will feel about your career when you're ready to retire or move on?

Are the differences between the two charts significant? What do those differences say about the kinds of legacies you're setting yourself up to leave? What do those differences say about the kinds of aspirations you've articulated in your legacy statement?

For many executives, the plate exercise bluntly illustrates the depth and breadth of their investment in activities that do not explicitly contribute to the kinds of legacies they want to create. The challenge, at least in part, then becomes organizational. Do your intentions align with your natural role, talents, and skills and yet you consistently engage in activities that don't play to those strengths or don't allow them to surface? If so, you need to rethink how you partition your time.

The plate exercise can also reveal a discrepancy between what you think you want (on the second plate) and what you really want. One manager, for example, told us that his initial second plate had a large chunk of unscheduled time. When he started thinking about ways to make that time available, however, he realized that he likes the speed at which he operates and the fact that his schedule is almost always at full capacity. He said, "I had some guilt, actually, that I was always doing so much, not taking time for other things. But the joke of it is that this exercise has helped me to understand that I like this pace. I don't want to slow down, at least not now."

Legacy thinking, and all the exercises related to it, is not a blanket call to stop and smell the roses. It can be, for some people—but for others it can affirm that there's tremendous value in experimentation or that they thrive on 24/7.

Once you believe in the honesty of your second plate, what do you need to do to get there? That's the topic we turn to next.

CHAPTER **6**

Are You Doing the Right Thing?

From Statement to Action, Audits, and Beyond

Men acquire a particular quality by constantly acting a particular way . . .
You become just by performing just actions, temperate by performing
temperate actions, brave by performing brave actions.

—Aristotle (384 BC–322 BC)

INDIVIDUAL LEGACIES CAN BE FORMED in an instant. A single interaction can have a lasting impact. In fact, it is likely that some of the legacies you would like to leave—legacies that are reflected in your legacy statement—are already taking hold among one or more of the people in your organization and beyond.

It is also possible, however, that among some constituencies, your influence is felt by certain people, but not to the extent that it affects their behavior; and some of your less desirable, unintentional legacies also may be forming. And it is possible that although you are forging many individual legacies, the collective impact that might be seen in a photomosaic is as yet unformed or too blurry to decipher.

Part of what unites all these individual legacies is the consistency of your approach over time. Consistency of influence over time minimizes negative, unintentional legacies and bridges the intentional points of impact, even when there is no direct connection. Consistency also leverages the value of the impact you've had on any one individual, increasing the odds of that impact resonating among others and affecting their behavior.

That kind of consistency—and the corresponding increase in the value of your leadership legacy—requires moving from statement to action. This chapter is devoted to helping you make the transition as explicit and straightforward as possible.

IDENTIFYING ACTIONS TO MOVE YOU
IN THE RIGHT DIRECTION

The first step is to reconsider the constituencies your leadership touches—successors, employees, colleagues, and so on, as described in chapter 2. As exhibit 6-1 illustrates, the goal is to deliberately influence the intensity of your impact on others across the greatest bandwidth. The most powerful leadership legacies are created at the upper-right end of the chart, where your intentional legacies influence the behavior of the greatest number of people.

EXHIBIT 6-1

Legacy impact chart

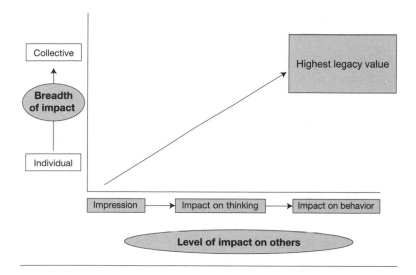

Using the "Stop, Start, Continue, Know, Do, Avoid" Framework

With those constituencies in mind, ask yourself, What specific actions should I stop, start, or continue in order to facilitate or strengthen the legacies I want to create? What do I need to know (where is my expertise, and what are my limits there)? What should I do (given my expertise, my natural role, the context of my position)? What should I avoid (what actions might be undermining my efforts)?

We often use the "stop, start, continue, know, do, avoid" framework when we prepare leadership development seminars for midlevel managers. We go to the senior managers and leaders in the company, and we ask them, "Knowing what you know

now, from your vantage point, if you were a midlevel manager in this company, what would you wish someone would tell you? What would you want to stop doing? What would you wish someone would tell you to start? Avoid? Continue?"

Their answers are usually heartfelt, because the template immediately prompts them to remember the more painful moments of their experience. As a result, the lessons that emerge to shape the seminars usually strike a nerve with the attendees.

The leaders' answers also reveal, in part, the way they want to see elements of their own legacies take hold. Here, the template serves almost the same purpose, particularly as you consider a newly written legacy statement, because it can help you expand and clarify the section that talks about how your legacies will be manifested.

The exercise is highly personal because it is inseparable from the particulars of your job. But following are examples of the scope and types of answers that will be most helpful. In this first pass, broad, general responses work well:

- You might use your natural role as a point of departure. If, for example, you are an ambassador, "start" might bring to mind the following: "Start thinking about places where it would be right for me to intervene. Where would such intervention be welcomed rather than resented?"

- "Continue" might yield thoughts such as these: "Continue building and maintaining my contact list. People come back into your life when you least expect it; who could help me here? Who could help the people I work with? What can I do to bring those parties together?"

- If you are an advocate, "stop" might include, "Stop being abrasive in my passion for my cause. I want to see this cause advance; here's how I think I'm hindering the process in spite of myself . . ."

- "Continue," for an advocate, might include, "Continue keeping my allies informed and committed. I haven't talked with so-and-so for a week; I need to update people more regularly."

- "Know" might include, "Know what success looks like" or "I need to know more about which battles to fight. I haven't stepped back to look at the big picture for a while."

- "Do" might include, "Do create interim benchmarks."

- A builder might want to "know" how to engage others—how to learn to express a vision in ways that others can understand, using their terms. A builder might want to "avoid" being so inflexible or uncompromising on details that she loses the bigger opportunity to create.

- A truth seeker might want to "stop" being judgmental on the way to discovering the truth. He might want to "continue" figuring out new ways to get a message across.

- A motivator might want to "avoid" trying to fit a square peg into a round hole. "Not every person, protégé, or contact is right for every favor I might have in mind."

- An experienced guide might "stop" trying to limit her breadth. Part of what makes wise ones attractive to others in the first place is their breadth; this exercise can offer the permission needed to let more of yourself show.

- An experienced guide might also need to "stop" counseling the people whose reliance is becoming annoying. Experienced guides have to be particularly mindful of their saturation points.

Homing In on Specifics

The next step is to turn all those broad indicators into three or four clear, concrete accomplishments you want to foster in the next six to twelve months.

Identify one or two short-term assignments, and one or two medium-term ones, that honor the longer-term vision. Keep them simple and straightforward. Here are some examples we've heard:

- "I've got to rebuild bridges with Mary. Find something to work on together. Figure out a way to let her know I'm over it."

- "I've really got to start the new-job-hunting process. I need to let a headhunter know I would be open to a conversation."

- "It's time to rewrite the letter to new employees. Tell them what I hope they'll achieve now that they are here, and what to do to make sure it can happen."

- "I need to be more tolerant of Stan. Give him the time of day. There's a reason he's in that job (even if I may not think he's great at it, others, whom I respect, do), and I need to try to remember that, as a colleague, he is on my side."

- "I need to sit tight, and offer no advice, in the first three minutes of any conversation."

These are not the kinds of items you'd spell out in your annual performance goals or put on a regular to-do list. Some elements might be linked to your formal annual goals, but these are different and, for the most part, not for public consumption (as in the "Stan" example).

Get out your calendar, your PDA, your time-management software—whatever—and go to the date one month from now. Jot down the short-term assignments. Go to a date three months from now, and jot down the medium-term assignments. Write something along the lines of, "Talk to Herbie about creating that new product for X."

One leader likes this approach, not because there is any magic in the ninety-day progress window, but because he sees it in his calendar regularly and it helps him keep his legacy in mind. You might even say that taking this step gives you thirty days or ninety days before you have to start feeling guilty.

MANAGING HIGH ON THE LEADERSHIP LADDER

One of the ancillary benefits to the know-do-avoid exercise is that it reveals, at least in part, the methods you employ to achieve results. Positive and intentional leadership legacies, it almost goes without saying, are best seeded in trusting environments where employees are voluntarily committed to the goals and require little policing to fulfill the responsibilities of their jobs.[1] What's surprising is how many times the know-do-avoid exercise illuminates certain relationships that are less trusting than you may have thought or hoped.

Consider the leadership ladder shown in exhibit 6-2. Fear, force, and coercion—the leadership "methods" on the lower rungs of the ladder—generally hark back to a less kind, less gentle age, when employees were watched carefully and were expected to do what they were told. As methods, fear, force, and coercion countenance little or no free will, creativity, or flexibility on the part of employees. Managing on these rungs is hardly a recipe for loyalty on the part of a workforce, but in certain eras or certain environments, leaders didn't necessarily want to invest time in instilling loyalty among employees.

In the middle of the ladder, the leadership style is not as immediately connected with physical or psychological intimi-

EXHIBIT 6-2

The leadership ladder

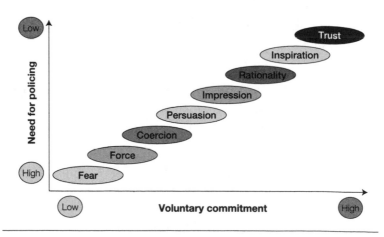

dation; here, less-threatening forms of ensuring compliance (or in more enlightened terms, securing alignment) come into play. In this group, leaders might use (and employees might respond to) persuasion, impression, or rationality as a means of achieving results. It is in this category that a change in employee behavior takes place, because if employees do something as a result of a leader's persuasion, impression, or rationality, then they are acting out of their own free will. They are making choices—not wholly without some influence by the leader (as in the case of persuasion or impression), but they are increasingly using logic as the basis of their decision making and behavior.

In fact, there is something of a breakpoint between the stage of impression (where a leader may exert some level of influence on an employee's thinking) and rationality, where employees have an unfettered understanding of the whys and wherefores of the leader's intention.

The highest categories, those of inspiration and trust, reflect an entirely different mind-set (and behavioral approach) on the part of followers as well as leaders. When people act or react on the basis of inspiration or trust, they are acting out of the highest intentions, and they work with greater levels of creativity and freedom.

It would be absurd to think that leaders and followers can always stay on that Utopian upper end of the scale. Sometimes we need to (or are forced to) step down a few rungs and use some of the more directive leadership behaviors. The critical issue, and the one that furthers legacy thinking, is the ladder elevation where a leader spends the preponderance of his time, and where he has the most memorable impact.

Where on the ladder do you spend most of your time? Consistent management at the low end can be a clarion call for coaching. But it can also be a signal that you might need to reconsider the fit between your natural role, the title you hold, and the legacies you'd like to leave. Managing on the lower rungs might indicate the presence of a level of strain that can greatly impede intentional legacies.

One consultant recounted the following story about recognizing her rung on the ladder and what it meant for her:

> I see that ladder and I think of the first significant project I had full responsibility for. I remember gathering the team at the initial meeting and telling them about the project, the goals, the timetable, what expertise each person was bringing to the table.
>
> I knew we had the right people to get it done. They were inexperienced; some of them were so young, it was probably their first project. But what we had to do really wasn't that difficult.
>
> Right at the end of the meeting I said something like, "I know we can do a great job on this." And then I said, "Just don't f*** it up."
>
> I remember right after I said that, the shocked expression on one woman's face, and the tense look on one of the guy's faces. I remember thinking, "Uh-oh. I shouldn't have said that." How scared they were! How nervous I was! To have put such pressure on them and to have set expectations in such a rigid, frightening way.
>
> I can look back on that now and understand that part of what I was feeling and how I was behaving stemmed from inexperience. But I can also look back and see clearly that I was trying to do a job that I really wasn't suited to do and did not, in fact, enjoy much. Thinking

about that job, and about other jobs I held, I see that I operated much "lower on the ladder" back then. I was me, and yet I wasn't, because my actions were driven by fear that I wouldn't succeed, and I turned that fear right around and used it to make people meet the standards I set . . .

All my life, I had been groomed, or "prepped," to be a leader. I remember family friends saying, "If she is as smart as we think she is, she'll grow up to run the country." I heard stuff like that—way out of whack with reality—all the time. And I know it set me up, at least in part, to be very hard on myself, very judgmental.

We didn't have as much money as a lot of the kids I went to high school and college with. We didn't have money problems that I was aware of, but my parents both worked very hard, and I always felt that I was the one who was supposed to get us all out of there (wherever "there" was) and move us to another level. I was ambitious. I got the early leadership positions. I fulfilled what I thought the expectations of those jobs were. I got good performance reviews. And I won't say that I didn't want to do all of that or that it was bad to do. But I knew at some level, even as I was moving up in organizations, that I didn't want to ever be fully in the driver's seat. I was always more comfortable as someone maybe near the top, but not the person with the final say on things.

Now, I can see that I had never stopped to listen to myself long enough to think about what I wanted to do. I didn't make time to stop and listen, and I was probably afraid of what I might hear. I remember asking a trusted family friend, at one point, "Would it be okay with the family if I just ended up working in a bookstore? Owning a little bookstore someday?" And I remember that she said, "Of course it would!"

But what I heard was, "Of course it would, if it's as big as Barnes & Noble."

It wasn't until I started raising a family that I started getting things straight. I explicitly allowed myself to understand that I didn't want the top job. During that time, I sought advice in ways I hadn't before. I remember one mentor said to me, "You're best when you're acting as the glue that holds the people in the organization together. There's a real need for people like that." She also said, "We're fortunate that we have choices. Choose how you want to spend your days, and tailor your job to that."

I came to realize that I was happiest when I was helping the people around me do "their stuff" better. Not when I was telling them what to do, but when they already knew what they wanted to do, and I could help them achieve their goals. To use the language of legacy thinking, I learned that there was too much of a conflict, for me, between the positions I had held and sought, and the roles that fit me best and brought me the most satisfaction.

I had a phone call two days ago—a former colleague offering me the top slot in a new venture. I told him no. I told him that I would be much happier—and could serve that organization much better—if I wasn't the headliner. My choice means less money, less recognition, less opportunity to be known as a leader.

I have absolutely no regrets.

BEATING (OR JOINING) THE GRIND

Mark Twain said, "Habit is habit and not to be flung out of the window by any man, but coaxed downstairs a step at a time." Manufacturers and retailers of exercise equipment tell us that there is about a ninety-day "window of use" for their products. After that, unless users have coaxed themselves to use the equipment a step at a time, the treadmill in the corner of the bedroom often becomes a metal frame for draping clothes. Ditto with New Year's resolutions, although the window of use on those is even shorter.

It's the same with legacy thinking. The sweeping goals can be inspiring, but the day-to-day effort is what yields the results. Emily Nagle Green of The Yankee Group put it this way:

> I find that the more I think about legacy as a tool, the more I come to understand that the question, "How do you want to be remembered?" really means, "How do you want to be thought of today?" That helps me put things in perspective.
>
> I've also come to understand more fully that we all have to get away from the illusion that a really good manager is one who has no weaknesses. If you want to design a meaningful legacy, you have to start with the inventory, whatever it may be. You have to be self-aware, and beyond that, you have to be authentic. Somehow, that makes it all easier to take.

This perspective is not at all new, except for the fact that we connect it to legacy thinking and draw the explicit link between attempting to build legacies and improving one's effectiveness as a leader. Much literature on leadership and management has stressed the importance of the day-to-day, in a variety of contexts. To draw on the work of Masakazu Yamazaki, consider this:

> To verbalize what those pessimistic and yet diligent Japanese may assert inwardly, one could perhaps say that we have no idea about the absolute and ultimate end of our lives, but we should try to live faithfully and elaborately each and every detailed phase of life as it unfolds around us. One could also say that since we cannot choose to achieve one single task that is central and essential to the meaning of our whole life, we should pour all our energy into day-to-day business.
>
> The wide acceptance of such a belief may be a particularly Japanese phenomenon, but the thesis itself is not the exclusive property of the Japanese. [Johann] Wolfgang von Goethe, one of the great thinkers of the West, was in part an agnostic himself, and he offered the following advice for those living under the burden of agnosticism: "How can one know oneself? By deed, not by meditation. Try to fulfill your obligations and you will at once realize what you are. What then are our obligations? Just those day-to-day things to be done."
>
> Goethe's words had a great impact on Mori Ogai, a leading intellectual during the early stage of Japan's modernization, when he himself felt that he had known no other norm for his life than "those day-to-day things to be done." He bequeathed to his family a household motto saying, "You should be able to be engaged in trifling things as if they were really enjoyable."[2]

All this supports the contention that it is critical to ensure, to the extent that you can, that the actions you identify are plausible and palatable. Ask of your action steps: Are they personally satisfying? Who wants to adhere to a list that forces you to address only unpleasant items? They should be objectives that you will feel good about completing—not just to get them off your list, but because they represent progress, or a new direction, or even a long-desired or dormant goal.

Ask also, of the broader, know-do answers, how often they might benefit from reconsideration and revision. You will probably want to look at them with an eye toward updating and revision every six months or so. That's expected and desirable. It is in the everyday, and in the day-to-day, that these things get built. But for most of us, the course of daily events means that our lives don't remain stable for very long.

THE LEGACY AUDIT

It is possible to define legacy goals that are realistic and achievable, that offer stretch and reach aspirations, and yet, for whatever reason, are not valued by those in your work environment. That's why the pressure test described in chapter 5 not only is useful the first time you do it but also becomes increasingly meaningful to conduct regularly as time passes.

When you first took the pulse of your legacy statement in terms of realism, achievability, stretch, and aspirations, your own critical eye, and the feedback you received from others, was based on your experiences before you engaged in legacy thinking. Now, having considered your work in light of the potential legacies you are forming, the reality check can become an increasingly accurate indicator of your progress.

Third-party feedback, in particular, becomes more valuable as time goes on. The people with whom you shared your initial legacy statement may be able to point to specific things you've done, or decisions you've made, that help or hinder your pursuit. New input from people who were not aware of your goals can show you whether the changes you've made or the steps you've taken have had a discernable impact beyond those in the know.

Two Kinds of Feedback

Sometimes this input must be solicited, as it is in the pressure test. But sometimes, gratifyingly, you may receive unsolicited confirmation that you are making progress.

An executive named George provides a good example. George had always been a high-strung leader. He found it almost impossible to delegate even the smallest tasks. He had to follow through on every little thing, all the time. When he began to engage in legacy thinking, the plate exercise, in particular, resonated with him. He realized that he spent a great deal of time following through on activities that, by rights, he shouldn't have had to follow through on.

George began the hard work of letting go. He reduced the number of times he checked in with people to whom he'd assigned a task or a project. He made it clear that he was there if they needed him, but he refrained from what he called "working over them."

Recently, he received some unsolicited feedback from an employee: "One of the things I like about working with you is that you let me show you what I can do." George, reflecting, said, "She didn't know me before. She thought this is just the way I am and have always been. I told her, 'It's something I work at,' and she seemed surprised."

Revisiting the pressure test seldom yields results as straightforward as this. Building legacies isn't like completing a connect-the-dots picture. But in the future, when you attempt to identify and supply evidence to support the theory that your legacy statement is right for you, it will be easier for you to do the exercise with confidence.

Peter Drucker's brilliantly simple and powerful feedback analysis can also be employed here:

> Whenever one makes a key decision, and whenever one does a key action, one writes down what one expects will happen. And nine months or twelve months later, one then feeds back from results to expectations. I have been doing this for some fifteen to twenty years now. And every time I do it, I am surprised. And so is everyone who has ever done this.
>
> Within a fairly short period of time, maybe two or three years, this simple procedure will tell people first where their strengths are—and this is probably the most important thing to know about oneself. It will show them what they do or fail to do that deprives them of the full yield from their strengths. It will show them where they are not particularly competent. And finally it will show them where they have no strengths and cannot perform.[3]

Not all the results of a legacy audit will be gratifyingly positive. As Drucker said about his feedback analysis, this type of review can reveal areas of perennial weakness. But if your goal is to make continual progress in creating your legacies, and improving your leadership in the process, then it's a necessary task.

Revisiting the Plate

Building leadership legacies is a dynamic process, and this means that your reflections on your priorities and your progress can't be static. That's why it's useful also to revisit the plate exercise after you've begun the move from statement to action. Even if you've managed to change a sliver of what you'd like to be doing into a slightly larger "small slice," you've made great progress.

In some cases, leaders can see measurable progress from their midterm accomplishments. Recall the leader mentioned in chapter 3, a man we call Matthew, whose schedule is so busy that it prevents him from mentoring developing managers as directly as he would like to. Matthew takes justifiable satisfaction in the internal management development program he has now commissioned and participates in. His current plate includes a sliver devoted to the kind of one-on-one time he wants to spend with the rising stars in his company.

In other cases, revisiting the plate after some time has passed causes a leader to seriously rethink the plans she originally made regarding her legacy. One print industry executive in her late thirties said this:

> I was off the mark. I was overly optimistic, or just not realistic enough, when I did this the first time. One of my strengths is that I can be very persuasive, so I convinced [the people she showed her initial statement to] that I could do it. Thinking about it now, I even made it seem

that I was on the cusp of doing all the things I set up to do anyway.

That really wasn't the case. When I looked at the plate again, I realized that it would take huge changes in the way I worked to accomplish the kinds of tasks I set for myself.

I was very discouraged, at first, when I realized that I hadn't made any progress. But then I started understanding that I was off the mark entirely the first time I went through the process. I was setting myself up for disappointment after disappointment. I am naturally hard on myself. I'm good at guilt trips. But I am starting to understand that if I'm not happy with the way I do things now, I'm certainly not going to be satisfied at the end of my career.

A close friend of mine had a cancer scare recently. The headlines in the news are starting to affect me more than they used to before I started this process. I'm doing the plate exercise again now and I'm trying to be more honest with myself about where I get satisfaction. I'm not as noble as I want to be; I get a lot of satisfaction from some of the more hard-nosed parts of my job. I thought I should be getting more satisfaction from the "softer" things. But that wasn't me. This is. I'm trying now to own up to the legacies I'm genuinely positioned to leave, and I'm trying to see how I can polish them up.

Legacy thinking, initially, can be a great exercise in delusion. But the follow-up hit home for me.

A few executives who reconsider the plate find that their priorities have simply changed in the past year and that the old plate

no longer applies. Interests have changed, new opportunities
have emerged, or personal issues have come to the fore. A senior
vice president in a large financial services firm told us this:

> In the last year, I have reached a point where, profession-
> ally, I really have no desire to continuously "do more," so
> I've tended to become less creative and less aggressive.
> No more tilting at windmills. Perhaps, as I intentionally
> slow my pace intellectually (if not physically), it will all
> catch up with me and come tumbling down, but c'est la
> vie. I'll figure out some new gig. The thing that doesn't
> change is my family and the loss of my nineteen-year-old
> daughter six years ago this month. My wife and I are try-
> ing to cope, and it has its ups and downs.
>
> I'm trying to define myself, these days, less by what I
> do and more by who I am—but this is a work in progress.

The plate exercise is not meant to serve as a judgment or an
excuse. It should not be used for either of these extremes. But
to the extent that it can heighten your awareness of yourself and
the path you are on, it is a good tool.

TANGIBLE SATISFACTION, INTANGIBLE RESULTS?

Moving from statement to action has significant personal implications. The process can be illuminating in small, positive ways
but also in large, wrenching ways. Our grief for legacies lost is
often our grief for things that never happened but should have
happened. What do the paths from statement to action reveal? Is
there a legacy to be built that you have yet to attempt? Recall

the words of U.S. Admiral Grace Murray Hopper (1906–1992): "A ship in port is safe but that is not what ships are built for."

In 2004 Michael Wiklund took action with a vengeance, leaving a secure job as head of the usability design practice of a major firm to open his own business as a designer and human factors consultant. His work for clients has included making surgical devices easier to handle, Web sites more attractive, TV and video remotes feel better in the hand, and even fireworks fuses safer. For the dozen years Rob (one of the authors of this book) knew him before this move, Wiklund had talked about going out on his own. There was usually a good reason that now wasn't the time or this wasn't the optimal moment: there was too much work, or there wasn't enough work. Yet Wiklund often spoke of how his potential, as a designer and as someone who could influence the industry, wasn't being explored; he felt sure it wasn't fully tapped.

He said, in an interview as this book was going to press, "I had always wanted to start my own company, and I spent a dozen years fighting against it." In the two years since he announced the decision, he has asked himself why he didn't do it earlier.

Barring unusual circumstances, you're better off being able to say, "Why didn't I do this earlier?" rather than, "Why didn't I do this at all?" Are the reasons that have prevented you from following a given path still valid? If you can't achieve the whole dream, can you achieve a part of it? Maybe you can't give up your high-paying job for full-time teaching, but might you be able to teach one course? What can you change about the situation to make your goal more achievable or bring it a little closer to reality? Without doing sophisticated forms of conjoint analysis, what compromises can you make that will help bring your legacy to life?

Just to drive the point home, consider Zach, who left a secure law practice, went out on his own in an investment business, and now owns eighty acres of vineyard in California. Enough said.

DIRECTIONAL, NOT DEFINITIVE

It's a wonderful thing when a legacy audit or a significant change in job or style yields specific, tangible signs of progress toward the building of a positive set of legacies. But there is no cause for alarm if you do not see these signs. Progress toward building successful legacies can often be found in more subtle measures.

An executive who runs the Asia practice of a large consulting firm said this: "We have lots of very smart people, and one of their tendencies at first is to do a great analysis and come forward quickly, demonstrating an answer. Over time we have to . . . show them that it is less about coming up quickly with an answer, and more about coming up less quickly with an answer that fully acknowledges the depth and breadth of the client's problem. Later in one's career, the approach is to listen to a client's problems and reflect on them more deeply before offering answers. It seems ironic, but we come across with greater wisdom when we don't have the answer at hand."

Progress toward building a positive set of legacies, or a coherent photomosaic, can be observed in the same manner. You might see it, not in your responses to things, but in an increased ability to hold back before you respond. You might see it, not in the things you are doing as a result of legacy thinking, but in the things that you are doing *less*. These measures, although less visible, are often profound. As William Schulz of Amnesty International offered, "The fact that a leader may not necessarily be identified with a single major accomplishment doesn't mean that the institution hasn't been stretched or made more healthy. It also doesn't mean that the leader doesn't have a vision. Powerful legacies can also be subtle."[4]

Russ Lewis, retired CEO of the *New York Times,* said, "I like to think that I'm fair-minded, that I have a balanced perspective and a sense of humor. It would be hubris to say that it has rubbed off on the organization. But to the extent that I try to be a decent human being . . . I think that encourages and plays to the better tendencies of the organization."[5]

Recalling the importance of the day-to-day, American writer and TV producer Norman Lear said, "You have to look at success incrementally. It takes too long to get to any major success . . . If one can look at life as being successful on a moment-by-moment basis, one might find that most of it is successful. And take the bow inside for it. When we wait for the big bow, it's a lousy bargain. They don't come but once in too long a time."[6]

The next chapter takes Lear's message to heart, and looks at legacy building in the context of the challenges and pitfalls that we all face at work.

Part III

Judgment

CHAPTER 7

The Need for Judgment

*Challenges, Pitfalls, Trip Wires,
and Other Bad Stuff*

HOLDING A SENIOR POSITION at almost any organization virtually guarantees that your efforts to build your leadership legacies will be fragmented and interrupted. But that statement isn't meant to discourage legacy thinking. Instead, it suggests that to be effective, your approach to building legacies at work must acknowledge and accept the fact that facing trip wires, pitfalls, and other challenges is an integral part of the process.

With that in mind, we introduce the final element of our definition of legacy: judgment. Judgment, over time and through conflict and threat, is the overriding factor that pushes legacies to reach their potential or, conversely, diminishes them or prevents them from taking hold.

Peter Drucker wrote, "Whether the compromise [a leader] makes with the constraints of reality—which may involve political, economic, financial, or interpersonal problems—are compatible with his mission and goals or lead away from them determines whether he is an effective leader."[1] This chapter examines the types of constraints of reality that can directly affect legacy building. It also suggests a way of considering the judgment calls you make in crafting compromises to navigate hazards successfully, leaving your legacies-in-the-making intact.

USING LEGACY THINKING
IN SPITE OF YOURSELF

Despite the proactive tone of this book thus far, legacy building is equally reactive. It is like driving a car. You may have a destination in mind, but many events—predictable and unpredictable—will influence the journey. You may have written as airtight a legacy statement as possible. You may have pressure-tested it thoroughly and emerged with an action plan as close to perfect as humanly possible. Then, just as you're gaining traction in integrating legacy thinking into your regular activities, you may find yourself dealing with the unexpected: mitigating a dispute with your board, for example, or snowed under by the details of an impending merger.

The natural reaction, under such pressure, is to push legacy thinking to the fringes as you deal with the short-term issues. The temptation is to forget that, with leadership legacies (as with driving), you reach the destination only by successfully navigating the road ahead, whatever surprises it holds. But just as it serves no good purpose to "forget" your destination when driving, it serves no good purpose to suspend your legacy-building activities while you're dealing with more immediate issues.

Recall the statement by Wendy's founder Dave Thomas that a reputation is earned by the actions you take each day. Here, as legacy thinking collides with the responsibilities of leadership, it is critical to remember that you build your leadership legacies minute-by-minute and day-by-day through the example you set, whatever the circumstances. You may not have control over the situations you face. What you do have control over is how you exercise your judgment as you face them.

We said in chapter 1 that legacy thinking is a tool or lens through which a leader's decisions can be filtered and assessed. We return to that theory here. Legacy thinking increases the odds that the judgment calls you make—whether they pertain to run-of-the-mill activities or crises—will result in satisfying outcomes for your organization and, in the process, foster your desired legacies.

DISTRACTIONS, DISRUPTIONS, AND DESTROYERS

No one is prepared for every hazard; no one calibrates every difficult situation with perfect judgment. But it is possible to predict and examine some of the more common types of events that can cause a leader to lose a legacy lens. By identifying and deconstructing certain types of judgment calls in advance, you can go a long way toward minimizing or avoiding damage to your intended legacy when the actual situation occurs.

Broadly speaking, the challenges leaders face as they integrate legacy thinking into their daily work can be sorted into three types: distractions, disruptions, and destroyers.

Distractions

Distractions are time-consuming but not critical. One example is unexpectedly having to take a half-hour to pacify a needy rainmaker. Another is the need to handle a growing volume of e-mails that take an extra minute or so each day. A third might be an unexpected call to weigh in on an ad campaign that is good, but not great. These events, by themselves, may not have any noticeable effect on your efforts to build a given legacy, but they can creep up on you. They can take time away from the kinds of activities that build your legacy. Recalling the plate exercise, you might find that your current plate is loaded with such distractions.

It is important to deal with distractions as if they were opportunities (however vexing) to exhibit the kinds of behaviors that support your intended legacies. But it is equally important to figure out as early as possible how to minimize the number of distractions you deal with daily.

Sometimes, distractions can be successfully countered with improved logistics. (Is your assistant really screening calls and e-mails appropriately, or managing your travel schedule in the most efficient way? Are you managing to avoid making constant eye contact with your BlackBerry while in meetings?)

However, distractions can also indicate that you aren't delegating the types of tasks or as many tasks as you should. Regarding your immediate colleagues and direct reports, to what extent can you rely on them to work with you, as opposed to simply working next to or below you?

This book isn't about organizational design. But we've found that the answer to many executives' problems in dealing with distractions often lies in the make-up of the group of people who surround them. Organizations may call this group the senior leadership team or the cabinet. We'll borrow from one organization we work with to call it the "eight to ten chairs."

Your eight to ten chairs typically include your key direct reports, along with a few people with senior-level responsibilities in other line positions. These are the people who deal with the many issues that are important to the smooth operation of the organization but are not necessarily central to either your position or your natural role. Maybe dealing with a rainmaker is important to the organization, but if it doesn't play to your natural strengths, then it is more likely to detract from, rather than contribute to, your efforts to build a legacy. It is here that you must bring to bear the self-awareness that grounds legacy thinking.

We know one executive—we'll call him Tim—whose eight to ten chairs were recently shuffled as a result of a division taking on new responsibilities. Previously, Tim's chairs were highly competent in their own rights, but not all of them complemented the styles of the others or of Tim. During performance reviews conducted just before the expansion, however, Tim had the opportunity to reflect on (and receive feedback on) the contexts in which he excels and in which he finds the greatest satisfaction. Now, in part as a result of those reviews, there are several new faces among the chairs. As a result, the whole team is better able to play to Tim's strengths and mitigate his weaknesses.

Distractions, if they're dealt with successfully, often don't even register as interruptions to legacy building. They're like twigs in a big river. As long as there are only a few, they don't noticeably affect the current. But the greater their number, the more likely there is to be a significant blockage. Distractions, unaddressed, rapidly escalate into disruptions.

Disruptions

Disruptions, as we've just noted, are sometimes the cumulative effect of distractions left unchecked. An unwieldy and unceasing log of e-mails might be one example. An untenable travel schedule might be another. A third might be a rainmaker who has become so dependent on personal counseling and feedback that whenever she isn't rainmaking, she seems to be demanding attention in person or sounding off on your voice mail.

Disruptions can be one-time events, or they can take such a significant chunk of your time and effort that they force a detour in your legacy plans.

The loss of a key senior executive might be considered a disruption. An operating failure in a division is another example, as are the slow erosion of the marketplace, a change in key industry players, or the loss (or addition) of a key customer. These events are not part of the norm of day-to-day operations, but they're not outside the realm of the generally expected realities of doing business.

Again, the important factor here is how you bring your judgment to bear on the situation at hand. As with distractions, a leader can either deflect disruptions, deal with them (and sustain a link to legacy building), or allow them to escalate to the next level. There's an old saying: "Man plans, and God laughs." The dynamic nature of building legacies is proven at this level, as a leader struggles to keep himself in view while handling these larger hazards.

At one company we know, the CEO—we'll call him Leon—is struggling with a disruption that seems likely to escalate. Leon's predecessor was beloved throughout the company. He has been gone for almost four years, but top executives still ask,

"What would Bill do?" They also shake their heads and say, "Bill wouldn't have approved of that" when a decision is handed down that they disagree with. They have come to respect Leon over the past few years, and the company has grown and prospered under his watch, but it has been difficult for this CEO to establish himself in a company where some employees still sort themselves according to whether they joined before or after Bill left.

Recently, Bill came out of retirement to launch his own firm, poaching several senior-level managers from his former company. The ensuing management churn has settled down, then escalated, and then settled down again, as the new firm plants flags in areas that have long been considered company strongholds.

Leon, the new CEO, has always had clear goals: he wants to take the company to the next stage of development and create a blueprint for the next type of firm in a rapidly evolving industry. In doing so, he wants to build an organization of forward-thinking managers. Leon has never been inclined to clean house; his style has tended more toward building consensus around his vision. Now, though, he seems to spend most of his time plugging holes where managers have left, trying to reassure managers who are staying, and trying to anticipate where the next managerial flare-up will occur. He keeps trying to galvanize his team by reiterating his vision. But what was a disruption is currently in danger of escalating to the point where this CEO's original goals and legacy hopes may be flattened. He is building leadership legacies, but, unfortunately, they are not currently the legacies he wants to seed.

There is probably no way that Leon can deflect or delegate the kinds of actions required to refocus his managers on the work of the company, and on his vision. So to salvage the essential themes and behaviors of his intended legacies, he may have to adjust, at least temporarily, his vision and strategy for the company. In chapter 3, we mentioned two executives whose visions and strategies (along with their desired legacies and natural roles) were put on the back burner as they dealt with organizational dysfunction. Leon will have to do the same thing, working on parallel tracks to end the growing internal crisis.

Legacy thinking isn't about being true to yourself and your goals while the company collapses around you; it is about handling your responsibilities as a leader so that your own values and philosophies remain intact. Think of refueling an airplane in midair; it's a similar concept.

Destroyers

Destroyers are often disruptions that have spiraled out of control. But these giant hazards can take several other forms. For example, they can come from left field, in the form of major events or crises, perhaps magnified by media attention. An alleged accounting scandal might be one example. Another might be accusations of a tainted product (as in Wendy's experience with the fraudulent claim about its chili, discussed in chapter 1).

Much has been written in general leadership books about handling such crises; best-practice advice suggests that gathering facts quickly, accepting responsibility, and making your actions and reactions as transparent as possible are the fundamental tenets of getting through these difficult times intact.[2] The same sort of advice can be applied here, with the caveat that legacy thinking binds you to factor in your own strengths and weaknesses along with the example you hope to set (and feel you can set) as you go forward.

The most insidious legacy destroyers are those that are seeded internally, recognized, and unfortunately left to grow. These destroyers are rooted in the fundamentals of legacy thinking. Misunderstanding or denying your natural role eventually catches up with you. Similarly, ignoring strong indicators from the outside also catches up with you. In chapter 3, we discussed how to assess whether your role and position are aligned. We talked about considering the marketplace demand for the behaviors you want to build your legacies on. The results of these assessments become increasingly important as time passes.

Consider exhibit 7-1. Plotting the dimensions of demand and desire against each other provides a quick check of whether

EXHIBIT 7-1

The demand–desire trade-off

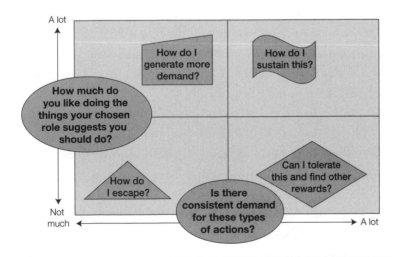

you are currently operating in an environment that is likely to permit you to succeed in developing your legacy. It would be a wonderful world if there were always a great demand and great appreciation for the work we love to do, but we don't always have that luxury. There are times when the demands of your work require you to focus your attention elsewhere, and other times when the work isn't very interesting. If large gaps or trade-offs persist and widen between the behaviors you want to build your legacies on and the demands for those behaviors, it is likely that your intended legacies are not taking root. At such a juncture, you have a decision to make about your work, your job, or your career.

Consider the sample of a manager we'll call Phil. Only in his thirties, Phil is on the senior leadership team of a global manufacturing company. He has recently received some stark feedback from his peers and direct reports about his management style.

Phil has always been a great go-to guy; his bosses have always given him the toughest projects, and he has always tackled them, conquered them, and delivered the hoped-for result, albeit leaving a wide swath of destruction in his path. His nickname, fully earned (and stemming from his military training), is "Take-the-Hill Phil."

The problem is that Phil has now reached a management level where his take-no-prisoners approach doesn't work. The command-and-control model that seemed to serve him well as he leaped up the corporate ladder now hinders his further advancement.

Phil was made to understand, through the feedback he received, that if left unchecked, his style would reverse the upward trajectory of his career at the company. He took the feedback stoically, but later he admitted that he was shaken by the fact that his approach, on which he had built so much success, was no longer going to work.

But he also understood why his approach could not work at this company at the senior level, and so he decided to try to change.

Some six months into the change effort, what is helping him the most, he says, is almost a cookbook of behaviors he has collected and refers to constantly as he works. Reduced to its essentials, the cookbook is a list of simple guidelines, such as "Ask people what they think" and "Don't cut people off when they're talking." He referred to them daily at the beginning of this process; now he doesn't rely on them quite so much.

Phil recognizes that these changes do not touch the talent that he brings to bear on the organization; nor do they keep him from making decisions that are his right to make. Instead, these new behaviors allow him to build and sustain the kinds of bridges he will need to work effectively, long-term, at the more senior levels of the corporation.

But as Phil has said in his blunt way, "This is very hard for me. I really need to keep thinking about how to do this step by step, especially the 'soft stuff' that I have always avoided." He adds, reluctantly, "But I know it is necessary."

Phil acknowledges that if he doesn't make an effort to change, he will probably continue to be assigned increasingly higher hills to conquer. He also understands that at the same time, if he doesn't change, he will close off opportunities to choose those hills himself.

What he hasn't yet considered is whether, in the long run, the effort to change such a fundamental part of his nature will serve him well. Currently, it seems that the legacies he is seeding are unintentional, and somewhat negative. Continued success at this company is certainly possible for Phil; the monetary rewards are already great. But at what personal price?

The jury is still out on the eventual outcome of Phil's effort. But consider two other examples, which illustrate the dangers of staying a course that you're not ultimately suited for.

From an early age, Shannon has had a spiritual side. She faithfully attended religious services in an era when regular churchgoing was not a typical teenager's habit. Shannon seemed genuinely interested in religion. Her parents, on the other hand, always wanted her to be a doctor. They weren't shy about it. They made it clear from an early age. Being a dutiful daughter, Shannon was a premedical student as an undergraduate, ending up at a distinguished liberal arts college. There, she ran headfirst into religion courses that nearly threw her off course. Her interest and attention to those offerings were immeasurably greater than her attraction to organic chemistry and the sciences. She openly discussed how much she loved the religion courses and how she longed to attend divinity school and pursue a career as a minister or a religion professor. It probably would have suited her perfectly, and those around her knew it.

Perhaps because blood is thicker than water or because parental influences are not always escapable, Shannon ended up as a doctor. But she wasn't a very happy one. Today, almost thirty years later, she has a good reputation as a competent, careful practitioner, and she has found a certain satisfaction in her work, but medicine was never her calling, or even a strong interest. Shannon still laments the choices she has made. She believes that she could have made a greater difference in the world and could have been a much more satisfied person had she followed her passion. What will her legacies be? To those who know about her regrets, at least one of Shannon's legacies may be a poignant message to follow one's heart when it comes to choosing a career.

In the second story, we have Steve, who started work at age eighteen as a blue-collar employee of a large manufacturing company. Steve worked first on the line and gradually, over twenty-five years, as a line supervisor, shift supervisor, and factory foreman. In the entire time Steve has been at the company, he has been something of a fish out of water. The manufacturing industry where Steve has worked has a macho culture and heritage, and Steve is not a macho guy, either in stature or in culture. He is loyal to a fault, hardworking, diligent, and well intentioned, but he is too neurotic, territorial, and hesitant to be viewed as a dynamic leader or role model.

Eventually, after numerous changes in the scope and scale of the business, it has become clear that Steve has been Peter-Principled up the ladder as far as possible and that a larger foreman role is now beyond him. At this point, Steve has been employed by the company for more than thirty years, and he has openly expressed a desire to complete thirty-five years of service before retirement. Rather than fire him, Steve's benevolent employer has put him into a corporate staff role, heading up a number of administrative functions.

As one might imagine, Steve is floundering there as well. He's overwhelmed by the complexity of a position that years ago would have been fairly routine but is now far more fluid, and far more high profile, than ever before. Steve continues to struggle, suspicious of any inroads onto his turf. His colleagues tolerate him in his administrative role, but they work around him, ignore him, or "dis" him. The administrative areas in his purview are substandard, and only now is the organization beginning to address the issue head-on, largely under the guise of a corporate reorganization, still leaving Steve with a number of departments under his control.

What will Steve's legacy be? It is clearly an unintended (and unfortunate) one, of someone who is out of his league, who has tried hard but just doesn't have the bandwidth to grow and change.

Could this have been prevented? Should his employer have kept him on? Would a "tough love" conversation have helped? Would Steve have had the courage to change, or to leave earlier in his career, if he had been given the message? These questions underscore the importance of thinking about what you are suited for and whether, by considering your legacy (and encouraging others to do the same), you might help people lead happier, more productive lives. Certainly, at least one doctor (Shannon) and at least one manufacturing foreman (Steve) might have fallen into that category if either of them had taken their inner voice to heart earlier.

Russ Lewis, formerly of the *New York Times,* summed it up well when he said, "The earlier you can be true to your understanding of who you are, no matter where you are, the more satisfied you are likely to be, and the more satisfied those around you are likely to be. At the very least, you will feel a lot better about yourself."

THE LESSER LEGACY

If you talk with highly successful people, those who appear by all external measures to be "Masters of the Universe" (or some vague equivalent) and who have it all, you know that they actually don't. They talk about how they could have done more, or they lament that their work was incomplete, or they express personal regrets that will remain unresolved. All of us, even the most successful among us, find ourselves dealing with the thought of leaving less-than-perfect legacies, although their value will vary by degree.

For example, consider Sue, who found herself at the helm of an HR department that had to make staffing cuts three times in eighteen months. Sue thought that there would be only one round of layoffs. The subsequent surprising cuts have caused her to believe that she has created, at least for some, an accidental and regrettable legacy. (Her method, as she dealt with the second and third rounds, however, likely underscored the straightforward way in which she deals with crises; there may be a positive legacy stream in that case.)

Jerry provides another example. Hired by a well-capitalized energy venture funding group, Jerry soon found himself spending the better part of two years selling off businesses when the parent company decided to exit certain competitive arenas. He lamented the change, saying, "I came in thinking I would be like an obstetrician, and it was more like two years working in a hospice." No doubt the legacies he formed while in that position were triggered by external circumstances. A few of his more general legacies from that period were likely negative; however, he probably also formed some meaningful, positive legacies because of the careful and sensitive way in which he managed the divestitures.

Jeff Nelson, at this writing a pitcher for the Texas Rangers, offers a more public example, albeit outside the realm of management. As a New York Yankee in the 2003 season, Nelson was one of the participants in what has become an infamous brawl. In a *Boston Globe* article published late in the 2004 season, he expressed frustration at the circumstances that had Red Sox fans booing him on the field. Here's an excerpt:

> "Look, this is a great place," [Nelson] said. "I love coming here. The fans, the rivalry between the Yankees and Red Sox is great. The atmosphere here is fine. I don't mind it.
>
> "It's just unfortunate that I'll only be remembered for [the fight]. It's tough because you've always got to think about it now. As much as I've done in my career, it's a shame, because people will only remember that one incident. That's what you're labeled now and that's the hardest part to ever get over, because they say, 'There's the guy who was in that incident, that stuff in the bullpen.' They don't remember what you did as a pitcher, and it's not like I was a scrub. I was used all the time."
>
> Nelson believes there's a simple reason the incident escalated to the point it did, with criminal charges levied. It was the "NY" on his cap. That wouldn't have happened, he said, if he had been pitching for the Mariners or the Rangers.
>
> "All they see is the NY," he said. "It's a shame. I have a family. I do a lot of charitable things. My dad is a cop, a retired Maryland state policeman. I've been in the game 13 years. I'm not some rookie or a thug or a guy with a history of yelling at fans. I've yelled at some umpires, sure. But other than that, I haven't done anything at all.
>
> But I'm forced to pay for it because of the NY, not because of the person."

The courts ultimately will assign blame. In the meantime, Nelson said, he has not heard anything from the Sox. "The only thing that night, John Henry [Red Sox principal owner] came out and said, 'We're supporting our people.' That's a joke, too. I'm not a bad guy. If I had a history of doing that, fine, but I don't. I didn't hear anything from them, no 'I'm sorry it happened.' Do you think if I was a Mariner or a Ranger when that happened, that they would have made this big a deal of it? Absolutely not.

"Will it ever go away? Who knows?"[3]

Sometimes there's nothing you can do. You may always feel as if you've been tagged, in the public eye, with a negative legacy as a result of one incident that may not reflect your genuine personality, ethics, or way of being in the world.

In an unfortunate case like that, your only recourse is to try to accept the fact that the passage of time is your friend and that the importance of this particular legacy will fade. In the case of Jeff Nelson, for people who aren't interested in the doings of the Red Sox or the Yankees, the incident probably never even registered.

The photomosaic keeps growing, surrounding the negative legacy with others you can see and direct more clearly. Over time, this one tile, or section of tiles, hopefully will be rendered insignificant. When we look at a wide swath of negative-turned-positive experiences among public and private figures, three clear and common themes emerge that bear on the legacies these people have built.

First, these leaders are dedicated and unflagging in their desire to learn from their experiences. This is true if we look at masters of invention (such as Andy Grove, the influential former CEO of Intel) or reinvention (such as Michael Milken), or even if we look at less-celebrated examples of those who have been affected by other events, perhaps even of their own making.

Consider Enzo, a former colleague of Rob's (one of this book's authors). Enzo, a partner in a large consulting firm, was flamboyant, charming, and impeccably dressed, and he had a variety of ex-wives and girlfriends. On many occasions, both at work and away from the office, he displayed a surprising insensitivity to those around him.

Rob hadn't heard from Enzo, or thought about him, for years. Then, out of the blue, he got a call from him. Enzo said, "I have been doing some thinking. Tell me honestly, was I mean to you when you worked for me?"

The answer, honestly, was, "Yes, I guess I'd have to say you were."

Enzo's reaction was one of surprise; he seemed almost incredulous. But he immediately apologized and soon thereafter ended the call. Rob next encountered him at a funeral several years later, where they acknowledged one another, but Enzo seemed to want to avoid conversation.

It's possible that Enzo called Rob as part of a passage of self-discovery. Something may have happened in his life that caused him to reflect, suddenly, on his past behavior. Rob doesn't know. What he does know is that for him, Enzo's legacy has changed. "I don't remember him, anymore, as only being brash and insensitive," Rob says. "I remember him as being thoughtful, and possibly regretful. His legacy to me, today, is a reminder of the possibilities of turnaround."

Second, people in this category are efficient mourners. They have a way of dealing with—not denying—reality and then moving on. They spend limited time on recrimination and little time on rationalization and trying to clear their names. (In fact, unless they have committed a crime or an act of notoriety, the brush of publicity will wear off before the next big news story overwhelms it.)

Monty provides a good example. His story hinges on the success he has achieved after dealing with his alcoholism and its effects on family relationships, as well as a career that has been stymied by corporate mergers and acquisitions. Monty did pretty well into his early forties—top-school MBA, a good (but not spectacular) professional career, followed by a migration into a senior staff role. Then it all fell apart; the organization, which had been his professional home for almost twenty years, was changing. Monty was perceived as part of the old regime. He was probably viewed as a somewhat tired horse in the role, although at that point he was only in his mid-forties. His job fell apart, and at the same time his marriage ended. To Monty's credit, he was able to move on and reinvent himself.

He has built his recovery on his own set of observations and experiences, which he has woven into powerful stories. He has written about his recovery, speaks about it, includes it in his work, and applies it in his daily life. He is happier and more successful now than ever before. It has taken him almost ten years to get there (although he may argue it has taken a lifetime, and it's still not over). Monty's desire to learn from his experiences, and to keep learning from them and adapting them, has been a critical element of his success.

Finally, such leaders are willing to alter their paths. Michael Milken, whose spectacular successes as a financier have been chronicled almost as much as his legal challenges in their wake, managed to turn his considerable assets, efforts, and energies into a significant force in, among other things, educational advancement and the fight against prostate cancer. Whether or not you are a fan of Michael Milken, the ultimate impact of his philanthropy in those areas, and on philanthropy in general, cannot be understated.

All this doesn't imply that when you are faced with a defeat, you need to change course completely. After all, Michael Milken did have substantial financial resources to ease his transition. But a willingness to change fields is not just a last resort for these people.

Professor Emeritus Renato Tagiuri of Harvard Business School put it well when he said, "As you relinquish one dream a little, you can then start considering alternatives. I can think of a situation where working with a senior colleague, you realize you have certain aptitudes or qualities because that person says so, and in the process you realize that maybe you don't have other aptitudes or qualities. And that is a positive traumatic experience. You have to decide when to jump. You have to try to turn the perspective from 'I'm unhappy here' or 'This isn't right, yet I must make it work,' to 'This is a good place to jump *from.*'"[4]

CHAPTER **8**

Legacies and the Responsibilities of Leadership

Your Duty to Enable the Legacies of Others

THE BULK OF THIS BOOK is devoted to helping senior managers think through the legacies they want to create in the context of their work and their natural roles. The emphasis is largely personal, focusing on aligning the kinds of legacies you are seeding with the kinds of legacies you want to seed. We've talked about how legacy thinking—the process of trying to build legacies proactively, as opposed to reflecting on them after the fact—can be a useful tool to help you factor your own personal satisfaction, strengths, and weaknesses into the decisions you make at work, to the benefit of the organization.

We've drawn an analogy between a leadership legacy and a photomosaic, the idea being that the streams of influence that you have on individuals throughout the organization and beyond, taken together, can form a coherent and positive whole, reflecting your best-practice behaviors and views.

This chapter adds a final element to the mix: the additional legacy that senior managers should be seeding as part of their responsibilities as leaders. The chapter then explores a few ways in which leaders can check on their legacies in progress.

THE LEGACY THAT LEADERSHIP SHOULD REQUIRE

In chapter 1, we cited John Kotter's definition of the responsibilities of leadership: vision and direction, alignment, and motivation. As we've discussed, legacy thinking does not directly affect the quality of your vision and direction, although it can bring clarity to those elements of leadership through your enhanced understanding of your own intentions, motivations, and abilities against the backdrop of the company's competitive position, its capabilities, and the marketplace.

Legacy thinking does, however, link directly to alignment and motivation. As you learn more about how your behavior influences those around you and come to perceive which streams of influence you want to emphasize, your understanding of interpersonal dynamics also deepens.

Because you're a leader, though, the benefits—and responsibilities—shouldn't stop there. It is one thing to try to ensure that your own best practices are passed on and adapted by others. It is equally important to help others in the organization gain from the same level of self-awareness. Only in helping others seed their own legacies can your positive influence reach its full potential.

Farmers understand this concept well. If you can get good crops from the soil every year, great. But the long-term value of the farm lies in the land's ability to continue to produce long after a given farmer is gone. The net value of the farmer, then, comes in the ability to maximize the rate of production without scorching the earth.

Parenting provides another good analogy. To the best of your ability, you provide for your children those things that they need to grow and thrive while they're directly under your care. You want to instill in them the best parts of yourself and your judgment so that when they become independent, they'll be ahead of the curve. Ultimately, however, the goal is for them to develop their own strengths, using what you've taught them as a foundation on which they can build their own paths and forge their own happiness, interests, and successes. That's a parent's net value.

It's the same with the net value of a leader:

Good: Providing a period of good performance and high returns

Better: Instilling the best elements of your leadership in others

Best: Helping other people in the organization deliberately create their own legacies and thereby ensure that they can in turn perpetuate their own best practices

A reflection by Australian Prime Minister Robert Menzies (1894–1978) is apropos: "A man may be a tough, concentrated, successful money-maker and never contribute to his country anything more than a horrible example. A manager may be tough and practical, squeezing out, while the going is good, the last ounce of profit and dividend, and may leave behind him an exhausted industry and a legacy of industrial hatred. A tough manager may never look outside his own factory walls or be conscious of his partnership in a wider world. I often wonder what strange cud such men sit chewing when their working days are over, and the accumulating riches of the mind have eluded them."[1]

Consider, too, what Harry Levinson noted, writing about the perspective of IBM founder, Thomas J. Watson, Jr.: "Neither size nor present demand for the company's goods and services is a real indication of its capacity to survive. The capacity for perpetuation lies in continuous regeneration. Contemporary behavioral science . . . shows that there is indeed the possibility of a 'fountain of youth' in organizations. Organizations can create social and psychological climates that are conducive to the creativity and flexibility of organization because they permit the people in them to grow."[2] To our minds, that fountain of youth is located where legacy thinking meets and joins the ability to foster in others a similar enhanced self-awareness and consideration of the long term.

How do leaders make this happen? The direct answer calls for leaders to encourage legacy thinking among their immediate colleagues and, in doing so, encourage those colleagues to do the same with their own direct reports, and so on. Reduced to specifics, this task can seem hopelessly detailed and complex. But even though the investment in self-reflection and legacy thinking is significant, the point of the exercise is to make your work easier in the sense that it fits more seamlessly with who you are to begin with. So when you take seriously the concept of legacy thinking, the ripple effect—fostering legacy thinking in others—can be one of the natural outcomes.

Sally Green of the Boston Federal Reserve Bank, reflecting on legacy thinking two years after she first participated in a multiple perspectives exercise, put it this way:

This isn't a tool that you sit down with and deliberately use to direct your interactions with other people, or affect your decisions. You don't end up saying, "What's going to be my legacy as a result of this action, or this statement, or that conversation?"

But once you've spent some time with the concept, it keeps bubbling up. All of a sudden you'll think, "There's a dimension of this issue, or decision, or conversation, that's important to me and to others on a deeper level, and that could also have long-term implications." Or, "There's a chance here to do something good for the long term as well as for today."

As you're working, you then begin to get a better sense of the managerial pipeline, through legacy thinking. That instinct, or knowledge, can help you help others find out where they can excel and find their greatest contributions.

Putting it another way, if you don't know where you're going, what's the point in energizing people? And once you know where you're going, it's critical to be able to mobilize people, to excite them, to get their juices flowing towards a common purpose. But it's a much better thing to have them be able to do the same for themselves—to think strategically, to align with the vision, and excite all their coworkers. Legacy thinking, it seems, is about succeeding and being satisfied with the kind of success you've achieved. What can you give the people you work with so that they can also be successful and proud of what they have accomplished?[3]

There's an old joke about an ant and a centipede walking along. The ant asks the centipede, "How is it that you can keep all those legs coordinated as you walk?" And the centipede, who until that moment had been swinging along just fine, stops to consider which foot goes first and which foot goes next, and soon he falls flat on his face, his legs hopelessly tangled. The same concept applies to legacy thinking and the responsibility of a leader to help others seed their own legacies. If you try to deconstruct it too much or connect the dots too specifically, the task becomes hopelessly complex. But if you allow the essence of the concept to permeate your thinking and your actions, the process can become an integral part of the way you work.

LEVERAGING YOUR SUCCESSION PLAN

To consider this concept from a slightly different angle, place it in the context of succession planning. The additional responsibility of legacy thinking is to help build a community of future leaders who are capable, self-selected, and able to perpetuate the concept.

Why "community"? Why not "group" or "stream" or "network"? We say "community" because it implies interdependence, complementary strengths and interests, and an agreement between people who may differ significantly and have different interests to come together and build something for a greater good.[4]

Think of a small town. Think of storekeepers, who may have disparate interests and beliefs at the personal level but nonetheless respect one another. These are people who say things like, "Can you make change?" "Will you watch my store for a few minutes while I go to the bank?" They care about one another and share a mutuality of interest in the town's well-being. They have also self-selected; they're in business in that location because they choose to be.

A community of future leaders is much the same. It starts with the idea of a company that has a strong leader and a number of skilled senior managers, each of whom might be able to take command one day, and then it ratchets this concept up a notch. A legacy community is also a skilled group, but these folks understand that even though their own opinions might differ regarding how the company should be run, and even though their own personal priorities, strengths, and weaknesses may differ, they have deliberately selected the organization they're in. They know that it is their *duty* to reach a meeting of the minds at a higher level and to work as a united front against the competition and for their employees.

Again, as with the ant and the centipede, it is not worth the effort to map the minutiae of execution. But we offer a few broad examples of the ways in which this responsibility plays out.

Firing People

The primary reason people get fired is that they're failing in their jobs. The act of firing someone is often traumatic to the point that people avoid or defer the responsibility as much or as often as possible. But if you couch the act of firing people in the context of getting them on their way to find a place where they'll succeed, it becomes less traumatic, and you clarify the right approach to doing it. In the process, you also open up an opportunity for another individual, who may be more suited to excel in your organization.

The Downstream Effect of Empowerment

Maria Feicht, a marketing executive with the Bertucci's Italian restaurant chain, told us about her own career, specifically in the context of someone at a different company for whom she had worked long ago. Feicht said that this person had always given her challenging assignments and had always exhibited the utmost confidence in her ability to handle the tasks. That confidence—which came in the form of comments like, "Thank you for taking this on; I'm here if you need me, but it's good to know the project is in your hands"—meant a lot to her then but has come to mean even more in the years since. "Knowing that someone who you respected believes in you, even if you haven't worked for them for a long time, helps when things are difficult later on," she said. "It helps to be able to dig down and retrieve it, and it gives you some confidence at those tougher moments. When I began to realize that I drew on that confidence, even years later, I began to try, deliberately, to have that same attitude and approach with the people who work for me. My sense is that it makes for a stronger organization."[5]

Encouraging People to Surpass You

In "Motivation and Productivity," Hiroshi Takeuchi wrote, "Salaried workers in Japan have a saying: 'Be controversial in your twenties, but after you have passed your fortieth-year milestone, lose the argument.' In other words, young employees should argue aggressively with others to develop an under-standing of work, but by the time they are senior managers, winning an argument with subordinates only discourages the subordinates' will to work. Deliberately losing an argument to subordinates encourages their will to work and thus benefits the company."[6]

Take the essence of that short excerpt and consider the comments of Alice Milrod, whom we described in chapter 2:

> If you believe in this community of future leaders con-cept, then encouraging people to surpass you isn't an option; it is a requirement. A woman who worked for me once observed that I always hired the best people I could get. She said it didn't look as if I was afraid to be out-stripped in terms of capabilities. She said I was always try-ing to push people beyond my own limits, and she asked me why I did that. Talking about one employee in par-ticular, whom I had helped take a step up, though it meant moving him to another department, she said, "Why would you ever give that person up?" And I said, "Because I had to. I wasn't being forced to, but how could I not?" It was so clear this person was ready to take on something new and bigger.
>
> I don't look to be remembered for my work. Big organizations forget about people when they're gone; it's like footprints in the sand—a wave comes in and they're swept away. So what it's about, in the end, is the inter-personal relationships and the careers I might have affect-ed and helped build. To have someone say, "She helped me step up," is the most I could hope for.[7]

Jay Westcott, a senior partner of WilmerHale, put it this way: "As you advance in your career, after a while, you are likely to have made all the contributions to the body of knowledge that you can. You may have written a definitive contract or brief, and that is important, but ultimately it isn't going to feel like enough. So the enduring value that you have, the most meaningful legacy you can render, is that of developing others—lawyers, younger partners, and so forth."[8]

WHAT DOES SUCCESS LOOK LIKE?

What does successful legacy thinking look like? Can it be measured? Are there any indicators to look for? No one would want to discover a stream of a leadership legacy in the way Fred Sturdivant did (as described in chapter 1): by hearing himself mentioned at the funeral of a young colleague. But there are several ways you can assess the depth and breadth of your legacies in progress.

Internal Indicators

One of the most direct ways to take the pulse of your legacies is to use Peter Drucker's feedback analysis technique, as described in chapter 6. Another is to revisit the plate exercise to see whether, over time, you've been able to close the gap between your first and second plates (or whether, in fact, the contents of your second plate have shifted at all). As we mentioned earlier, one company president, upon revisiting his plate, realized that, for him, the downtime he had originally thought he wanted on his plate wasn't what he wanted at all; his real desire was the taxing 24/7 schedule he already had. Revisiting the plate exercise relieved him of a lot of guilt.

A third possibility is to take a few moments to consider three or four of your recent decisions in light of legacy thinking to see whether they sit well with you. Consider the situation in which an executive was fired for abusing the company credit card. One of the senior managers who had a hand in the decision, and who has been engaging in legacy thinking, noted this:

> When this situation came up, the knee-jerk reaction was to fire this manager abruptly. We've always made it known throughout the company that any violation of the company code of ethics would result in termination. But the more I considered that option, the more I thought that a public, and therefore deliberately humiliating, dismissal wasn't the right course. We had insight into this manager's personal situation; this person is the sole supporter of a family; imagine the effect on them if the scandal were deliberately made public.
>
> In the end, we allowed him to resign. And it gives me pause that we did that. Our objective was to be fair to everyone, and it may seem that we weren't. But I'm thinking more long-term these days than ever before, and I think that this was an instance that called for fairness with compassion. It's known through the company why this executive left. These things get out; we knew that the gossip mill was churning. But by allowing him to resign, we didn't compound the problem—which is already so serious—for the family.
>
> It feels more right than wrong, the way we handled it. Long-term, it feels right, personally, and for the company.

And it feels more in keeping with the person I try to be outside the office; with the person I try to be with my own family. Fairness with compassion in this case stayed true to our zero tolerance policy, but in a humane way.

Abraham Maslow's Theory Z also factors in here. As a commentary in Maslow's book, *Maslow on Management,* notes: "Theory Z presupposed that people, once having reached a level of economic security, would strive for a life steeped in values, a work life where the person would be able to create and produce. Although Maslow died before finishing his work with Theory Z, we see evidence today that his theory was several decades ahead of its time."[9]

Reflecting in general on your work life, some months into the process of legacy thinking, are you better able to identify the areas that give you the most satisfaction? Francis Bonsignore is a forty-year senior executive in human resources in the financial services industry and the former chairman of the Employee Benefit Research Institute. He put it this way:

> I think that a lot of how one views oneself early in one's career has to do with how well accepted they are in their institutional setting. You're looking for approval from the company, or the organization. As you get older, and as you accumulate experiences, both good and bad, that kind of institutional legitimacy has less to do with it ... The later in your career you are, the more you define yourself in personal terms, rather than in corporate terms ... Personal terms have everything to do with how others may move forward because of their contact with you. Maybe you

made a difference in the body of knowledge; maybe you've challenged conventional wisdom somehow. Your contribution will really only be seen in the actions of the people who follow you. The thing about legacy thinking is that it can expedite that process of self-discovery.

I hope people will look back on me and say that I was a partner in the best sense. I hope that they'll say I really had something worthwhile to say. But I'd like to think that they'll say the same thing I hope my kids will say: "He made me aware of things, and stressed things, that are now a part of my world view."[10]

External Indicators

Reflecting on your legacies in progress can be gratifying and also useful. But it is equally important to look for external cues that you're moving in the right direction. Most performance reviews concentrate on tangible achievements in hand. These are lagging indicators, and even though they're important, they tell only a part of the story: what you have done.

With legacy thinking, it is equally important to look for leading indicators, which project future accomplishments: what your actions will do.

Ask yourself, Has this organization increasingly become an exporter of talent? What is the recruiting climate like? Check recent employee surveys, beginning with data from the people who work directly with you. What is the tone? Has it changed or evolved in any way? In these measures you can see legacy thinking that is starting to have teeth. Ultimately, it can also become part of the fabric of the organization, part of its culture.[11]

A CAUTIONARY TALE

The work of building intentional legacies is never done, even if legacy thinking becomes an integral part of the way you work. The following story underscores that fact.

Lawrence is in his fifth year as CEO of the one-hundred-year-old, $5 billion "PrintFilmedia" Corporation. Lawrence was the first outsider to be hired directly as CEO. He brought to the firm a top-tier MBA, a considerable amount of indirectly related business experience, and the gold-plated resume of a twenty-five-year career.

Although Lawrence did not come with the standard film or technical credentials that were the backbone of PrintFilmedia's core business, he was and is highly regarded as a strategic thinker. For the most part, his lack of technical expertise and directly related business experience has not detracted from his overall effectiveness, although it has been periodically noted by the other home-grown, long-tenured line executives when contentious decisions are afoot.

As a strategist, Lawrence has aggressively (and successfully) expanded the definition of PrintFilmedia's core business and value proposition, helping to protect its reputation and standing as the industry leader in North America. This expansion has come from a mix of home-grown entry into ancillary businesses as well as a modest amount of small, highly opportunistic acquisitions. Slowly Lawrence appears to be building a team of like-minded visionaries; this is an important legacy for him.

In the most recent expansion (or rather, expansion attempt), however, Lawrence encountered, for the first time, a level of resistance that has given him (and the entire PrintFilmedia organization) no small measure of concern regarding his ability to lead.

Lawrence brought to the attention of the organization a potential acquisition that, as a firm, was riding the crest of a new set of technical standards that was likely to affect the film industry in the years ahead. The target firm was considerably ahead of any competitors and had established a well-developed set of contacts and contracts with key purchasers that gave it a large, highly defensible market position. The head of the target firm, however, was cut from a different cloth than most PrintFilmedia managers, and that factor, among others, contributed to the storm of opposition that all other members of management (except Lawrence) raised against the deal.

Even though Lawrence presented clear logic and a good strategic rationale and the proposed acquisition represented a relatively modest financial risk, members of the senior management team balked at the deal. Their comments:

"The way that company does business, with their adversarial, combative approach, indicates that they are not our kind of people."

"We have no one who could run that business if the current CEO bolts."

"We're already behind on our annual plan. This acquisition will be a huge distraction to our achieving the plan."

"Instead of spending the millions on this deal, why don't we invest it in our own business growth?"

These members of Lawrence's leadership team admitted that Lawrence had made a fundamentally logical case for the acquisition. But their resistance was strong and sufficiently broad. Ultimately, Lawrence backed away from the deal.

On one level, this is a disappointment given the deal's intrinsic logic and attractiveness. On a more profound level, Lawrence is concerned that he wasn't able to convince his fellow executives of the acquisition's value. He is even more concerned that his leadership team in effect vetoed his recommendation. This might have been an appropriate decision-making protocol in a partnership, but in a traditional corporate structure such as Print-Filmedia's, it has certainly given the impression that Lawrence can be overruled by the rest of his management team.

Initially, the conflict over this acquisition could have been called a disruption, but it escalated to the point where it was a potential destroyer. Managers who had previously seemed enthusiastic about Lawrence's forward-thinking approach began to say things like, "Lawrence has a huge vision, but we have limited resources. We can't keep expanding without shoring up internally."

What it probably says—and what Lawrence is realizing—is that he may not have taken the same level of care to operate high on the leadership ladder in this situation as he has in the past. Blown away by the logic of this opportunity, as it appeared to him, he forgot, in the process, that his senior leadership team was just starting to come along in thinking about the longer-term possibilities for the industry and for the company. Lawrence acknowledges, reflecting on this issue, that in large part, he bypassed the careful steps he took to build consensus and even let others drive the enthusiasm for earlier deals.

THE POWER OF POTENTIAL

When considering the concept of legacy thinking, Harvard Business School Professor Emeritus Renato Tagiuri said, "Day to day you have fifteen things to do, and you will do three, maybe five of those things. You will choose to do those things based on some criteria. Why not add to your criteria what you would like your legacy to be? If you can do that, and you are clear about it, it will provide a rudder for those around you."[12]

Barnes Boffey is one of the senior officers of The Aloha Foundation, a one-hundred-year-old nonprofit educational organization based in Fairlee, Vermont. Aloha oversees the operation of a variety of programs and camps that offer educational programs for adults, children, and businesses. He is an exemplar of Tagiuri's simple and profound perspective on legacy thinking, and we close this book with a few of his colleagues' comments, and with his own words. Boffey participated in the multiple perspectives exercise a few years ago. His third-party respondents wrote, among other things, the following:

> He has given me a philosophy, through his own behavior, that I can pass along. He has given me something to aspire to and something to teach. As a result of working with Barnes, I try to teach people that there are better ways to lead in this world. He has inspired me to be better, and he has helped me walk my truth as a psychologist. I say to people, "As a leader and as a person, you can help create an environment where you can tell me your truth." The thing about sharing this; it can sound so clichéd. But Barnes knows how to do it.
>
> —*Larry Larson, consulting psychologist who also maintains a private practice. Larson also conducts leadership workshops with organizations in the United States, Canada, and Australia.*

Barnes's legacy to me centers around an ability to frame the most difficult situations—work or personal—into a set of simple choices. As a result of having worked with him, I'm able to turn even situations that seem at first overwhelming into a set of choices that feel more manageable. Barnes taught me not just to go with my gut, but *how* to go with my gut.

—*Bryan Partridge, professor, New England College.*

Barnes is modest about his own achievements and humbled by the comments others have made about his leadership. But that doesn't diminish his belief in the importance of legacy thinking. As he puts it, "Our lives are not exercises from school that have no relevance. In fact, they have the ultimate relevance. Our lives can damage other people; our lives can heal other people; our lives can nourish other people, and our lives can transform other people. Our lives become the stars that others steer by, and if we live them well, the world will change."[13]

It is hard to imagine a more powerful leadership legacy for each of us to pursue.

Notes

Chapter 1

1. Vijay Vishwanath and Marcia W. Blenko, "Inside Kraft's Leadership Corridor," *Leader to Leader* (Fall 2004): 27; and "The Art of Developing Leaders at Kraft," *Harvard Management Update,* November 2004.

2. Roger Lang, interview with Rob Galford and Regina Maruca, December 2004.

3. Dan Ciampa and Michael D. Watkins, "The Successor's Dilemma," *Harvard Business Review,* November 1999.

4. John P. Kotter, *John P. Kotter on What Leaders Really Do* (Boston: Harvard Business School Press, 1999).

5. Jack Schuessler, "Food for Thought," *New York Times,* May 17, 2005, A12.

6. Fred Sturdivant, interview series with Robert Galford, 2003, 2004, March 2005.

7. Roch Parayre, speaking at Merrill Lynch, July 2005.

8. George Colony, interview with Regina Maruca, March 2004.

Chapter 2

1. Emily Green, e-mail interviews, Spring 2004.

2. Roy Schifilliti, interview with Regina Maruca, May 2004.

3. Michael Porter, "Clusters and the New Economics of Competition," *Harvard Business Review*, November–December 1998.

4. Ralph Nader and William Taylor, *The Big Boys: Power & Position in American Business* (New York: Pantheon Books, 1986), xii.

Chapter 3

1. Alice Milrod, interview with Robert Galford, February 2004.

2. Sally Green, interviews with Robert Galford and Regina Maruca, June and September 2004.

3. Jim Rossman, interviews with Robert Galford, March 2004 and April 2006.

4. Tom Leppert, interview series with Robert Galford, 2004, 2005.

5. Ibid.

6. Russ Lewis, interview with Regina Maruca and Robert Galford, July 2004.

7. Rob Cosinuke, interview with Regina Maruca, June 2004.

8. Randy Myers, "A Dying Breed," *Corporate Board Member,* March/April 2004; "Corporate Jungle May Claim Another Victim," *Financial Times,* October 20, 2003; "Do You Need a COO?" *Healthcare Executive,* July 2002; "COOs Become Obsolete as Corporations Reorganize," *Pacific Business News,* March 25, 2005; *Crist Associates' Volatility Report,* 2005.

9. William Schulz, interview with Regina Maruca, February 2004.

Chapter 4

1. Julia Boorstin, interviewer, "The Best Advice I Ever Got," *Fortune,* March 21, 2005, 100.

Chapter 5

1. Warren Bennis, *On Becoming a Leader: The Leadership Classic— Updated and Expanded* (New York: Perseus Publishing, 2003), 50–51.

2. Rob Cosinuke, interview with Regina Maruca, June 2004.

Chapter 6

1. Robert Galford and Anne Seibold Drapeau, *The Trusted Leader* (New York: Free Press, 2002).

2. Masakazu Yamazaki, "The Impact of Japanese Culture on Management" in *The Management Challenge: Japanese Views*, ed. Lester C. Thurow (Cambridge, MA: MIT Press, 1985), 37.

3. Peter Drucker, *The Essential Drucker* (New York: Collins, 2001), 218.

4. William Schulz, interview with Regina Maruca, February 2004.

5. Russ Lewis, interview with Regina Maruca and Robert Galford, April 2004.

6. Quoted in Warren Bennis, *On Becoming a Leader: The Leadership Classic—Updated and Expanded* (New York: Perseus Publishing, 2003), 51.

Chapter 7

1. Peter Drucker, *The Essential Drucker* (New York: Collins, 2001), 270.

2. Ronald Heifetz and Marty Linsky, *Leadership on the Line* (Boston: Harvard Business School Press, 2002).

3. Gordon Edes, "A Range of Emotions for Texas," *Boston Globe,* September 5, 2004.

4. Renato Tagiuri, interview with Robert Galford and Regina Maruca, February 2004.

Chapter 8

1. Robert Menzies, *The Columbia World of Quotations* (on Bartleby .com), 39309, 1996.

2. Harry Levinson, *Executive: The Guide to Responsive Management* (Cambridge, MA: Harvard University Press, 1982), 93.

3. Sally Green, interview with Robert Galford, February 2006.

4. Jay W. Lorsch and Thomas J. Tierney, *Aligning the Stars: How to Succeed When Professionals Drive Results* (Boston: Harvard Business School Press, 2002).

5. Maria Feicht, interview with Robert Galford, February 2004.

6. Hiroshi Takeuchi, "Motivation and Productivity," in *The Management Challenge: Japanese Views*, reprint edition, ed. Lester Thurow (Cambridge, MA: MIT Press, 1987), 22.

7. Alice Milrod, interview with Robert Galford, 2004.

8. Jay Westcott, interview with Robert Galford, September 2003.

9. Abraham H. Maslow, *Maslow on Management,* revised ed. (New York: Wiley, 1998), 72.

10. Francis Bonsignore, interview series with Robert Galford, 2004.

11. Lorsch and Tierney, *Aligning the Stars: How to Succeed When Professionals Drive Results.*

12. Renato Tagiuri, interview with Robert Galford and Regina Maruca, February 2004.

13. Barnes Boffey, interview series with Robert Galford, January and February 2004.

Index

About the Authors

ROBERT M. GALFORD is a managing partner of the Center for Executive Development in Boston. He divides his time between teaching executive education programs and working closely with senior executives at the world's leading professional and financial organizations on the issues that lie at the intersection of strategy and organization. He has taught executive programs at the Columbia University Graduate School of Business, the Kellogg Graduate School of Management at Northwestern University, and most recently at Harvard University.

Earlier in his career, Rob was executive vice president and chief people officer of Digitas (NASDAQ: DTAS), a marketing services firm based in Boston, with offices worldwide. He was also a vice president of the MAC Group and its successor firm, Gemini Consulting, focusing largely on the strategic and organizational challenges facing *Fortune* 100 companies, international financial institutions, and professional-services entities. While there, he worked for a number of years in Western Europe before returning to the United States, where he took on a variety of administrative and managerial responsibilities. He has practiced law with the international firm of Curtis, Mallet-Prevost, Colt & Mosle in New York and has also worked in investment management for Citicorp in New York. In addition, he has taught management policy in the MBA program at Boston University Graduate School of Management.

Rob is a five-time contributor to *Harvard Business Review,* including "When an Executive Defects" (case comment, 1997), "Why Can't This

HR Department Get Any Respect?" (1998), and "What's He Waiting For?" (2004). His work has also appeared frequently in the *Boston Globe,* where he has served as one of the regular "Job Doc" advice columnists in the *Sunday Globe.* He has been featured or quoted in such other publications as *Inc.* magazine, *Sloan Management Review,* and the *American Lawyer.*

Rob is coauthor of *The Trusted Advisor* (with David Maister and Charles Green), initially published by Free Press/Simon and Schuster in 2000 and subsequently reissued in paperback by Touchstone/Simon and Schuster in 2001. *The Trusted Advisor* has remained on business best-seller lists since its publication. His subsequent book, *The Trusted Leader* (coauthored with Anne Drapeau), was published by Free Press in January 2003.

Rob currently sits on the Board of Directors of Forrester Research, Inc. He also hosts the business video "Talk about Change!" with Dilbert, the popular cartoon character.

Rob's educational background includes Liceo Segre, Turin, Italy, a BA in Economics and Italian Literature from Haverford College, an MBA from Harvard Business School, and a JD from Georgetown University Law Center, where he was an associate editor of the *Tax Lawyer.*

Rob can be reached at rgalford@cedinc.com.

REGINA FAZIO MARUCA is a writer and editor based in Sandwich, Massachusetts. She specializes in books and articles that focus on leadership, marketing, and organizational issues. Her clients have included Bain and Company, Accenture, and McKinsey & Company. She has worked with a variety of distinguished authors, including Monica Higgins, Sam Hill, Edward Lawler III, Jay W. Lorsch, Paul Nunes, John Peterman, Thomas Tierney, and V. Kasturi Rangan. Most recently, she served as editor of *What Managers Say, What Employees Hear: Connecting with Your Front Line (So They'll Connect with Customers),* published by Praeger in 2006.

She is also a principal at the Center for Executive Development in Boston, where she helps develop curricula for executive training programs.

A veteran journalist, Regina is a former senior editor at *Harvard Business Review* and former associate managing editor at the *Boston Business Journal* and *New England Business* magazine. Her byline has appeared in those publications and others, including *Fast Company* and *Value* magazine.